mission-shaped church

mission-shaped church

church

church planting and fresh expressions of
church in a changing context

CHURCH HOUSE
PUBLISHING

Church House Publishing
Church House
Great Smith Street
London SW1P 3NZ

ISBN 0 7151 4013 2

Published 2004 by Church House Publishing
Fourth impression 2004

Copyright © The Archbishops' Council 2004
Index copyright © Meg Davies 2004

GS 1523

Cover design by Church House Publishing
Typeset in 10/12 Franklin Gothic

Printed in England by The Cromwell Press Ltd
Trowbridge, Wiltshire

Tel: 020 7898 1594; Fax: 020 7898 1449;
Email: copyright@c-of-e.org.uk.

Unless stated otherwise, Bible quotations are from
the New Revised Standard Version of the Bible
copyright © 1989 by the Division of Christian
Education of the National Council of the Churches
in the USA. All rights reserved.

*This report has only the authority of the Council that
approved it.*

contents

foreword

In the short – but not exactly uneventful – time during which I have been Archbishop, I have regularly been surprised and deeply heartened by the widespread sense that the Church of England, for all the problems that beset it, is poised for serious growth and renewal. Many feel that, as various streams of development over the past decade or so begin to flow together, we are at a real watershed.

The essence of this is in the fact that we have begun to recognize that there are many ways in which the reality of 'church' can exist. 'Church' as a map of territorial divisions (parishes and dioceses) is one – one that still has a remarkable vigour in all sorts of contexts and which relates to a central conviction about the vocation of Anglicanism. But there are more and more others, of the kind this report describes and examines. The challenge is not to force everything into the familiar mould; but neither is it to tear up the rulebook and start from scratch (as if that were ever possible or realistic). What makes the situation interesting is that we are going to have to live with variety; the challenge is how to work with that variety so that everyone grows together in faith and in eagerness to learn about and spread the Good News.

If 'church' is what happens when people encounter the Risen Jesus and commit themselves to sustaining and deepening that encounter in their encounter with each other, there is plenty of theological room for diversity of rhythm and style, so long as we have ways of identifying the same living Christ at the heart of every expression of Christian life in common. This immediately raises large questions about how different churches keep in contact and learn from each other, and about the kinds of leadership we need for this to happen.

All this is explored in these pages with a wealth of local detail and theological stimulus. This will be a wonderful contribution to thinking about how we respond creatively to the really significant opportunities and new visions that are around, and the Church of England owes a great debt to Bishop Graham and his working group for giving so penetrating and exciting an introduction to the possible shape of our mission in the next generation.

✠ **Rowan Cantuar:**

the *Mission-shaped Church* working group

Mission-shaped Church is a report from a working group of the Church of England's Mission and Public Affairs Council and is commended by the Council for study.

membership of the working group

Rt Revd Graham Cray (Chair), Bishop of Maidstone.
Revd Moira Astin, Team Vicar of Thatcham, Diocese of Oxford, and member of Board of Mission to 2002.
John Clark, Director, Mission and Public Affairs, Archbishops' Council.
Ven. Lyle Dennen, Archdeacon of Hackney, Diocese of London.
Revd Damian Feeney, Team Rector of Ribbleton, Diocese of Blackburn.
Canon Robert Freeman (Secretary), National Evangelism Adviser, Archbishops' Council, Archdeacon of Halifax from September 2003.
Revd Sally Gaze, Team Rector of Tas Valley Team Ministry, Diocese of Norwich.
Revd Graham Horsley, Secretary for Evangelism and Church Planting, Methodist Church.
Revd George Lings, Director, Church Army Sheffield Centre.
Canon Chris Neal, Formerly Director of Evangelization and Rector of Thame, Diocese of Oxford. International Director for Mission Movement, Church Mission Society from May 2003.
Gill Poole, Church Mission Society Area Team Leader.

a note on the discussion questions

It is hoped that *Mission-shaped Church* will be studied and discussed at diocesan, deanery and parish level. As such, *Mission-shaped Church* will necessarily have a number of different audiences. However, the questions that follow each chapter are intended for use by local leadership groups and can also be used by other parish or local fellowship groups. Groups do not have to use all the questions and may choose whichever seem most appropriate for their group make-up and context.

The first question in each group of five is of a general, philosophical nature and is intended to aid discussion or brainstorming surrounding the underlying principles of mission-shaped church. A suggestion for a passage of Scripture is included so that groups can focus the discussion down into Bible study if they so wish.

The second question also deals with the general principles underlying the chapters, but invites groups to take these principles and apply them to their local context.

The third question in each group is designed for people who like to make lists, draw diagrams or compose tables in order to think about issues or to think strategically about mission.

The last two questions in each group invite people to focus on the text itself. Groups are invited to engage directly with assertions or arguments in each chapter and to decide how these apply to their local situation. By this means, groups are further invited to explore what missionary strategy, church planting or fresh expressions of church might be most appropriate in their own situation.

Further information and resources may be obtained from Anne Richards, Mission and Public Affairs Division, Church House.

introduction

by the Chair of the Working Group

Breaking New Ground: church planting in the Church of England was published in 1994.[1] It set out to recommend good practice for church planting, and to address difficulties raised by a small number of unauthorized plants. It was of particular importance as the first formal document in which the Church of England owned 'planting' as a missionary strategy.

In 2002 the (then) Board of Mission set up a new working group to review the original report, to assess progress and to consider new developments. In particular it was recognized that a variety of new forms of church in mission were emerging or being put into practice within the Church of England. The new working group was to review these 'fresh expressions of church'.

Breaking New Ground saw church planting as 'a supplementary strategy that enhances the essential thrust of the parish principle'.[2] Perhaps the most significant recommendation of this current report is that this is no longer adequate. The nature of community has so changed (and was changing long before 1994) that no one strategy will be adequate to fulfil the Anglican incarnational principle in Britain today.[3] Communities are now multi-layered, comprising neighbourhoods, usually with permeable boundaries, and a wide variety of networks, ranging from the relatively local to the global. Increased mobility and electronic communications technology have changed the nature of community.

It is clear to us that the parochial system remains an essential and central part of the national Church's strategy to deliver incarnational mission. But the existing parochial system alone is no longer able fully to deliver its underlying mission purpose. We need to recognize that a variety of integrated missionary approaches is required. A mixed economy of parish churches and network churches will be necessary, in an active partnership across a wider area, perhaps a deanery.

In addition, our diverse consumer culture will never be reached by one standard form of church. The working group has evaluated a wide variety of 'fresh expressions of church'. All have strengths and weaknesses, and none are appropriate for all circumstances. In particular the dominance of consumerism presents a major challenge to Christian faithfulness. What is acceptable and what is unacceptable about consumer culture? In what ways can we be 'in' a consumer culture but not be bound by its underlying values? What forms of church does this require?

We offer our findings to help dioceses, deaneries and parishes discern appropriate forms of mission for their varying contexts.

We have entitled this report *Mission-shaped Church*. This echoes two themes within this report: that the Church is the fruit of God's mission, and that as such it exists to serve and to participate in the ongoing mission of God.[4] The report is subtitled 'church planting and fresh expressions of church in a changing context', reflecting our ongoing and shared calling to embody and inculturate the gospel in the evolving contexts and cultures of our society.

We understand 'church planting' to refer to the discipline of 'creating new communities of Christian faith as part of the mission of God to express God's kingdom in every geographic and cultural context'.[5] 'Fresh expressions of church' are manifestations of this, but they also give evidence of many parishes' attempts to make a transition into a more missionary form of church.

The report begins with an analysis of the current cultural context of the Church of England's mission. It then outlines the history of church planting in England, with special emphasis on developments since the publication of *Breaking New Ground* in 1994. After addressing issues of definition, the report offers description and analysis of a number of 'fresh expressions of church' that have emerged in response to the changing missionary context. Following the description of the current situation, Chapter 5 offers a theological framework for the Church of England in mission. The remainder of the report proposes a missionary methodology for church planting and for the Church in mission, and makes practical recommendations for the future.

One of the central features of this report is the recognition that the changing nature of our missionary context requires a new inculturation of the gospel within our society. The theology and practice of inculturation or contextualization is well established in the world Church, but has received little attention for mission in the West. We have drawn on this tradition as a major resource for the Church of England.

Inculturation is central to this report because it provides a principled basis for the costly crossing of cultural barriers and the planting of the church into a changed social context. Church has to be planted, not cloned. At the same time, any principle based on Christ's incarnation is inherently counter-cultural, in that it aims at faithful Christian discipleship within the new context, rather than cultural conformity.

The gospel has to be heard within the culture of the day, but it always has to be heard as a call to appropriate repentance. It is the incarnation of the gospel, within a dominantly consumer society, that provides the Church of England with its major missionary challenge.

This report has had to balance conciseness and focus with the need to give a good overview of changes in society and of all that is developing in areas of planting and fresh expressions of church. There is much more that could be written, and additional material is available from www.encountersontheedge.org.uk. A selection of useful books and other resources is listed in the Appendix to this report.

This report has been both challenging and exciting in its research and production. The working group has greatly valued the opportunity to reflect on where and how God is at work in and through the Church, and how the Church can be encouraged and shaped best to proclaim and live the gospel afresh.

Help, guidance and encouragement have been received from many people during the development of this report. In particular we would like to express our thanks to staff at Church House, the Church Commissioners and across the dioceses, and to various consultants who have contributed to our thinking, including Bob and Mary Hopkins, Stuart Murray Williams, Michael Moynagh and Mal Caladine. We are also grateful to those who have shared stories with us and which form the illustrative material and our thanks go to Ian Dewar, Karen Hamblin, Mark Meardon and to Virginia Luckett. We would also like to thank the Church Army, which very generously released George Lings for three weeks to prepare a first draft of this report. We have also been helped by the active support of a variety of denominations and church streams from across the United Kingdom, who have freely shared their own thinking and insights.

We believe the Church of England is facing a great moment of missionary opportunity, and recommend our report for the consideration of our Church.

✠ **Graham Maidstone**
September 2003

changing contexts

This chapter outlines some aspects of the cultural, social and spiritual environment in which the Church of England ministers in the new millennium. It explores how we are called to be and to do church, and the benefits and disadvantages of existing Anglican expressions of church.

We face a significant moment of opportunity. Western society has undergone a massive transition in recent decades. We all live in a fast-changing world. As the Church of England aims to be a Church for everyone in the country, being truly among them as Jesus was with the people of his day (the 'incarnational principle'), the Church needs to respond to the changes in our culture. Thus it is important for us to see what our culture now looks like, so we can see the possible shape, or shapes, of church to which God is calling us. This look at culture now will also help connect church and gospel with the variety of people across England, and identify where, under Christ's lordship, we should live counter-culturally.

social trends in the last 30 years

Each year the Government publishes *Social Trends*. *Social Trends* brings together the conclusions from a variety of statistical surveys.[1] Some headlines from the 2003 version are outlined here.

housing changes

- While the population of the UK has risen by 5 per cent since 1970,[2] the number of households has increased by 31 per cent.[3] There are now more households, but they are smaller in size. The average size of a household is now 2.4 people, in 1971 it was 2.9.[4] This is mainly due to divorce, and delay in marrying. The implications of this for the housing market are dramatic, particularly in some parts of the country. For example, the number of owner-occupied dwellings increased by 38 per cent between 1981 and 2002.[5]

- People are paying more in real terms for their houses. The rise in owner occupation means that repairs and improvements are the responsibility of the occupier, rather than a landlord. This has led to the rise of DIY in the last three decades, which is often a Sunday activity.

employment changes, including the increase of women's employment

- Most people in their middle years work outside the home. In 2002, 91.8 per cent of men aged 35 to 49 were in work, and 78.1[6] per cent of women in the same age group. There has been a significant increase in the number of lone parent women working outside the home. In 1992, 18 per cent of lone women with dependent children were working full-time, but in 2002 it was 23 per cent. The change for lone women with children under the age of five is most dramatic: in 1992, 21 per cent worked; in 2002, 34 per cent were working either full- or part-time.[7]

- The hours worked have also changed. In 2002 most men worked about 40 hours a week, and most women in full-time work worked about 38 hours a week.[8] However, about 25 per cent of working men and 11 per cent of working women worked more than 50 hours a week. Fourteen per cent of those aged 35 to 49 would like to work fewer hours for less pay each week.[9]

- This means that many people have less 'free time' than in 1970. Weekends, especially Sundays, are now seen as family time. This is a big tension for Christian partners of non-Christians.

mobility

- Today people are vastly more mobile than they were even 30 years ago. Since 1971 the distance travelled each year on roads in cars or vans has almost doubled from 313 billion to 624 billion kilometres.[10] The average length of trips varies significantly by household income – 15.3 km for the richest 20 per cent and 6.7 km for the poorest.[11] We are all more mobile, but a number of factors – where we live, where we work and how well off we are – influence how far and how often we travel.

- These statistics are matched by the number of vehicles on the road. In 1971 there were just under 12 million vehicles on the roads; in 2001 it was just under 26.5 million.[12]

- Most families, apart from the poorest, have access to a car, and are ready to use it. This means that people are able to work further from home, at the expense of having a longer commuter journey. It also means that at weekends people are able to do things at a distance from where they live. In churches this can be seen in the phenomenon of 'church shopping'. Someone who moves to an area will check out several churches, not just the nearest.

- Another aspect of mobility is the way in which some people move in connection with their jobs. Increased mobility means that people are less likely to live in the same area throughout their lifetime, and now tend to live further from their relatives than previously.[13]

- However, more than half of adults see their mother at least once a week,[14] and 61 per cent of grandparents see their grandchildren weekly.[15] Visits to relatives are most likely at weekends, due to school and work commitments in the week.

- The distance from relatives varies with social class. People in the professional social class were least likely to have a satisfactory network of relatives.[16]

divorce and changes in family life [17]

- The divorce rate has gone up significantly in the last 30 years (62,857 divorces in 1970, 154,628 in 2001).[18] The proportion of separated and divorced people now stands at 10.6 per cent of the population of England and Wales.[19] In 1971, 1 per cent of men and 1 per cent of women were divorced, but by 2000 it was 8 per cent men and 9 per cent women.[20] Additionally, about 8 per cent of families were stepfamilies with dependent children[21] – the parents no longer appeared in statistics as 'divorced' because they had married again. Combined with the rise of cohabitation and the birth of children to never-married mothers, in 2001 the Census showed that 22 per cent of children in England and Wales live in lone-parent families, usually looked after by their mother. More than 1 in 10 other children live in stepfamilies, mainly with their mother.[22] The average age of women at the birth of their first child has increased by 1½ years since 1990 to 27 years in 2000.[23]

- The number of single people has risen dramatically – because of not marrying, or marrying later. In 1971, 24 per cent of the male population were single, in 2000 it was 34 per cent.[24] Some of this change can be accounted for by cohabitation but, even taking cohabitation into account, there is a real rise in the number of single people. In particular, the number of single men has risen from 3 per cent of households in 1971 to 10 per cent in 2000.[25] This is due to the later age of marriage, and the rise in separation and divorce.

- The implications of these changes in family life are that very many families will be involved in visiting absent parents, usually fathers, often at the weekend. This will inevitably make Sunday church attendance problematic.

- The rise in the number of single people, and the delay in having children,[26] means that there is a significant group of people in their twenties who do not have children, and so child-friendly activities (and, indeed, morning activities at the weekend) may not be something they can relate to.

free time and television

- Taking part in sporting activities, whether alone or as a member of a team or a club, is a popular way of spending leisure time.[27] Walking and swimming are the most popular, with 20 per cent and 15 per cent of the population participating.[28] These are often Sunday activities, and in particular children's sport often occurs on Sundays as well as Saturdays and midweek.

- The biggest change in leisure time in the past 50 years has been in the hours spent watching television. In the year 2000, adults spent an average of nearly 20 hours a week, just under 3 hours a day.[29]

a fragmented society

One key conclusion from these snapshots of British society is that we are living increasingly fragmented lives. People who have had a longer education are more likely to live away from their parents, and are more likely to be civically engaged (i.e. involved in community groups or local politics).[30] People from the manual sections of the community are more likely to live near family and less likely to join local groups. Young adults may not join local groups, but will have an active friendship network. In any particular town there are many people who will never meet, even though they live nearby. They get in the car to travel to see the people they know and so do not meet the people who live close to them.

When they do have time, those who live away from their relatives, or who have children who live with ex-spouses, will visit them. People no longer view Sunday as special, or as 'church time'. Children are much more likely to be playing sport than being in Sunday school or church.

the power of networks [31]

The Western world, at the start of the third millennium, is best described as a 'network society'. This is a fundamental change: 'the emergence of a new social structure'.[32] In a network society the importance of place is secondary to the importance of 'flows'.[33] It is the flows of information, images and capital that increasingly shape society.[34] It combines the spread of information technology with increased possibilities for personal mobility. It both enables and is driven by the global economy. Globalization implies a networked world: 'Globalization promotes much more physical mobility than ever before, but the key to its cultural impact is in the transformation of localities themselves.'[35]

One consequence is a comparative loss of local and national power. For example, jobs can disappear from a community as a direct consequence of decisions made on the other side of the world, in response to a downturn in the global market. This does not mean that the 'local' is no longer important, but it does mean that it is subject to considerable change and is less free to shape its own future.

The Internet is both an example of network society and a metaphor for understanding it. From one perspective the Internet has no centre. There is no one 'place' where choices are controlled. Everywhere is linked to everywhere else. Each person chooses his or her own route, with a search engine as the only pilot. Networks of relationships are formed in chat rooms around mutual interests. Friendships are maintained electronically. But it would be untrue to say that the Internet has no centres of power. There are powerful financial networks that have significant control, and particular places (including London) that are physical hubs for the global network. Economic interests and the divide between the technological rich and the technological poor create their own forms of inclusion and exclusion.[36]

Networks have not replaced neighbourhoods, but they change them. Community and a sense of community are often disconnected from locality and geography. A typical town will have an array of networks. Each school will have a network of the parents whose children attend it, as well as networks of the children themselves. Each workplace will have its own networks, according to who works with whom, and these networks may spread to key suppliers or clients of the firm. Some of the networks may be based around a locality, particularly among poorer people who are less mobile. For example, the residents of a social housing scheme may still have a network based on where they live, as well as reaching out to their local relatives. The neighbouring private housing estate may have no such local network, and a person moving there may find it hard to meet people until they go to a group that is the heart of a network, such as a Baby and Toddler group in the town. Another network in the town may revolve around the nightclub, or the Working Men's Club. Of course, any one person may be in several networks, but some people will now be in none – due to the collapse of the neighbourhood as a friendship base.

Ulrich Beck has observed:

To live in one place no longer means to live together, and living together no longer means living in the same place.[37]

And Martin Albow comments:

The communities of the global age generally have no local centre. People living in the same street will have fleeting relationships with each other, having widely differing lifestyles and household arrangements.[38]

Information and knowledge have speeded-up, shrinking the world, but these have not conferred a sense of community. In 1996 the Henley Centre commissioned research to discover with whom people thought they had most in common. Top of the list were those with the same hobbies, then family, then work colleagues. Bottom of the list were those in the same area and neighbours. Geography no longer seems to be the primary basis of community. People define their communities through leisure, work and friendships.

It is not that locality, place and territory have no significance. It is simply that they are now just one layer of the complex shape of society. It has been said that 'All boundaries are tenuous, frail and porous'.[39]

We live in a society that is both fragmenting and connecting at the same time. It is not healthy or possible to escape all sense of place. Few people belong to 'no place' – many now belong to a variety of 'places' simultaneously. The social and personal significance of the place where they live has diminished.

Greater mobility, freedom of choice, and the creation of identity and community around shared interests is the way of life of large proportions of the population, and is no longer the privilege of the very affluent. Part of the deprivation experienced by the poor is their exclusion from a mobile lifestyle.

Mobility has become a major marker of inclusion or exclusion. Those who cannot move increasingly identify their deprivation in these terms. They are 'stuck' where they live, and feel they cannot enjoy life or express themselves fully or get a good job without the ability to maximize the opportunities that are available to mobile people.

The gospel has to meet people where they are, before it can enter and affect their lives. The planting of churches among the mobile and among the poor is integral to the Church of England's mission. The scriptural command 'that we remember the poor'[40] is given to all Christians, and so it is incumbent on all churches exploring church planting or fresh expressions of church to consider God's call to the poor.

For the comfortable majority the current degree of mobility is a mixed blessing. It offers freedom at a price. The consequences of fragmentation are seen most clearly in the drastic decline in 'social capital'.[41] 'Without at first noticing, we have been pulled apart from one another and from our communities over the last third of the [twentieth] century.'[42, 43]

There are two distinct social processes at work here. Community is increasingly being re-formed around networks, and people are less inclined to make lasting commitments. While the two are not unrelated, the first is a change in the structure of community, with which the Church must engage. The second is a corrosive force that the Church must resist, because it undermines all forms of community. Contemporary initiatives to plant the church, or to express it appropriately within Western culture, will need to establish social capital: ties of loyalty and faithfulness through Christ.[44] Both the establishing of bonds within networks and the bridging between networks will be crucial.

fresh expressions of church

Breaking New Ground recognized that 'it is possible to see that it is networks which are now the communities to which we feel a predominant loyalty' and that 'human life is lived in a complex array of networks and that the neighbourhoods where people reside may hold only a very minor loyalty'.[45]

The implication was that churches needed to be planted into networks. In *Breaking New Ground* this was seen as an addition to the normal territorial parochial system. However, it is now clear that the relationship between neighbourhood and network is more complex. It is not sufficient to think of neighbourhoods being supplemented by networks, or of network churches as a supplement to geographical parishes. Not only are networks more dominant for many people, but parishes are not what they used to be.

The perception of the working group producing this report is that many of the fresh expressions of church, explained in Chapter 4, are connecting with people through the networks in which they live, rather than through the place where they live.

Both community and locality are multi-layered. Geographical parishes need to recognize that their boundaries are permeable, and welcome a partnership with other parishes, and with network churches. Only a mixed economy of neighbourhood and network, collaborating together over a wider area (perhaps a deanery), can both adequately fulfil the incarnational principle and demonstrate the universality of Christ's lordship in all expressions of society.

A story

In the town of Huddersfield and its two deaneries an expression of church has been planted called The Net – a church without walls. It was created as a partnership between a then curate, Revd David Male, and the diocese to which he is accountable.

The name reflects the intention to work only with networks of people. It has denied itself any neighbourhood clientele base or working of a patch. The networks include business colleagues, personal friendships, a joint love of a sport, or common leisure interest. From a team of 28 people from varying existing churches in the town, a witnessing and worshipping community of more than 60 adults and their children has grown up.

Various locations round the town are used as meeting places dependent on their function. Its members may come from up to 30 miles away, but this is not a form of church eclecticism. It reflects the distance people normally travel to Huddersfield to work, how they form relationships and find their leisure. It is an example of church being expressed around how people live, rather than around where they sleep.

Churches may already be responding to the network society, without being fully conscious that that is what they are doing. For example, the acknowledgement that Church schools are 'at the heart of the church's mission' is a recognition that the network based around the school (both its children and parents) is a key grouping that may be receptive to the gospel. For the network associated with a school, it may be best to offer and encourage the sharing of the gospel through services after school, or acts of worship within school, rather than hope that people will come to church on a Sunday.[46]

consumer culture

Western culture is not only a network society, but it is also a consumer culture. Where previous generations found their identity in what they produced, we now find our identity in what we consume. We have moved from a society that shaped its members primarily as producers – those who believed in progress and in producing something that contributed to the better life that was certain to come through education and hard work – to a society that shapes its members first and foremost by the need to play the role of consumer.[47]

> Where once Westerners might have found their identity, their social togetherness and the ongoing life of their society in the area of production, these are today increasingly found through consumption. It's not that companies are producing less, or that people no longer work. Rather the meaning of these activities has altered. We are what we buy. We relate to others who consume the same way that we do. And the overarching system of capitalism is fuelled by consumption, and geared to stimulating consumption.[48]

The core value of society has moved from 'progress' to 'choice' – the absolute right of freedom to choose. 'Choice lies at the centre of consumerism, both as its emblem and as its core value.'[49] In this society everyone becomes a consumer.

> The amount of money available to individuals for consumption varies enormously, but virtually everyone today is a consumer to some degree. The poor have fewer resources than the rich, most ethnic and racial minority groups have much less to spend than members of the majority, children have fewer means than adults, and so on, but all are enmeshed in the consumer culture. Even those who live on the streets survive off the discards and charity of that wildly affluent culture.[50]

Furthermore, everything becomes a consumer choice. Central to the future is the idea of 'personalized scale' – 'it must fit me exactly'.[51] The world will be organized around giving people the sense, or perhaps the illusion, that they can have whatever they want. In the future, this approach to life will not just apply to consumer goods – it will be applied to all aspects of life. It is predicted that by 2020 personalized scale will also apply to health care, educational provision, patterns of work, of association and relationships, and of course to religion.

> The sweeping changes in society . . . mean that we are more mobile, more urban, more individualistic and more critical than previous

generations. So religion is less likely to be a matter of culture and more one of choice.[52]

Consumerism will also affect the ways in which people evaluate truth claims. The way people think about shopping also becomes the way people think about 'truth'.

> When many voices can be heard, who can say that one should be heeded more than another? . . . When the only criteria left for choosing between them are learned in the marketplace, then truth appears as a commodity. We hear the people 'buy into' a belief or, rather than rejecting a dogma as false, they say they 'cannot buy' this or that viewpoint.[53]

It is important to distinguish between 'consumer society' (a term that describes the current shape of Western capitalist societies) and the ideology of 'consumerism' (which can be seen as the dominant idolatry of those societies). In one sense there is no alternative to a consumer society. That is what we are, that is where we are and that is where we must be church and embody the gospel. To fulfil our Lord's prayer for the Church (John 17.15-18) we are called to be church 'in' consumer society, but we dare not let ourselves be 'of' consumerism.

At its worst, consumerism creates a self-indulgent society.

> Pleasure lies at the heart of consumerism. It finds in consumerism a unique champion who promises to liberate it both from its bondage to sin, duty and morality as well as its ties to faith, spirituality and redemption. Consumerism proclaims pleasure not merely as the right of every individual but also as every individual's obligation to him or her self. . . . The pursuit of pleasure, untarnished by guilt or shame, becomes the new image of the good life.[54]

In this, the poor are those who cannot buy things. A consumer society excludes the poor.

> Postmodern society produces its members first and foremost as consumers – and the poor are singularly unfit for that role. For the first time in history the poor are un-functional and useless, and as such they are, for all practical intents and purposes, 'outside society'.[55]

A network and consumer society presents a particular challenge to Christian mission in general, and to questions of the missionary shape of the Church in particular. A network society can both connect and fragment. It can include and exclude at local, national and global levels. Mobility can provide freedom and opportunity, but it is also a force that destabilizes society by undermining long-term commitments.[56]

post-Christendom

The emergence of a network and consumer society coincides with the demise of Christendom.

> What is taking place is not merely the continued decline of organized Christianity, but the death of the culture that formerly conferred Christian identity upon the British people as a whole. If a core identity survives for Britons, it is certainly no longer Christian. The culture of Christianity has gone in the Britain of the new millennium.[57]

Much of Britain's self-understanding comes from centuries of Christian faith, but many in Britain now have minimal knowledge of the Christian faith. The Christian story is no longer at the heart of the nation. Although people may identify themselves as 'Christian' in the national census, for the majority that does not involve belonging to a worshipping community, or any inclination that it should. Many people have no identifiable religious interest or expression. Among some young people there is little evidence of any belief in a transcendent dimension. During the twentieth century Sunday school attendance dropped from 55 per cent to 4 per cent of children,[58] meaning that even the rudiments of the Christian story and of Christian experience are lacking in most young people. Our multicultural and multi-faith society reinforces a consumerist view that faiths and their differences are simply issues of personal choice, to be decided on the basis of what 'works' or makes you happy.

The consequences for a national church, used to operating among people and institutions on the assumptions of Christendom, are acute. The Church of England bases a significant part of its identity on its physical presence in every community, and on a 'come to us' strategy. But as community becomes more complex, mere geographical presence is no longer a guarantee that we can connect. The reality is that mainstream culture no longer brings people to the church door. We can no longer assume that we can automatically reproduce ourselves, because the pool of people who regard church as relevant or important is decreasing with every generation.

> The Church has got to realize its missionary responsibilities. We live in a society, whether that be urban or rural, which is now basically second or even third generation pagan once again; and we cannot simply work on the premise that all we have to do to bring people to Christ is to ask

them to remember their long-held, but dormant faith. Very many people have no residue of Christian faith at all; it's not just dormant, it's non-existent; in so many instances we have to go back to basics; we are in a critical missionary situation.[59]

This report believes that the beginnings, in the last 20 years, of church plants and fresh expressions of church represent the emergence of a diametrically different approach that is both theologically appropriate and strategically significant. Instead of 'come to us', this new approach is to 'go to them'. We need to find expressions of church that communicate with post-Christian people, and which enable them to become committed communities of followers of Jesus Christ. Then they, in turn, can continue to engage in mission with and beyond their own culture.

from 'where?' to 'how?'

So how can the Church of England rethink its mission?

Anglicans aim to follow the pattern of the incarnation – to be with people where they are, how they are. The word 'where' in that sentence suggests geography and territory – being in a particular place and location. In Britain today, it might help to say that we must be with people *how* they are. 'How' is a word that suggests connection beyond geography and locality – connecting with people's culture, values, lifestyle and networks, as well as with their location.

A geographical approach alone is not sufficient. Parish, by itself, is no longer adequate as the Church of England's missionary strategy. 'One size fits all' will not do. A mutual partnership of parochial and network churches, using traditional and fresh approaches, and sharing ministry in larger areas is necessary.

The diversity of fresh expressions of church in this report ranges in style of worship from the reinvention of the traditional to the highly innovative. The size of these expressions ranges from the tiny cell to the enormous gathering. Furthermore, the starting point in mission sweeps from relational evangelism to many forms of social engagement. Venues and meeting days are getting more diverse. This is a response to the sense that Sunday is no longer a 'church' day for our society, but rather a family day, or DIY day, or sports club day or whatever people choose to do. Some people may be keen to meet with other Christians regularly, but it is no longer feasible for them to do that regularly on a Sunday.

All these variables can be mixed and matched by local churches with the resources to do so, or they can be expressed across a diocese or deanery – by a policy of encouraging variety and recognizing gifting and divine opportunity. No one kind of worship can attract, much less hold, a major proportion of the varied population of this country. The Church will be able to reconnect with both society and individuals through a pattern of diversity and unity, rooted in the triune, endlessly creative, life of God. It is a pattern that looks ahead to the diversity, brought from all corners of the earth, that will be celebrated in God's eschatological reality.

The new is not necessarily better or more lasting. For neighbourhood and network we need 'forms of Christian community that are homes of generous hospitality, places of challenging reconciliation, and centres of attentiveness to the living God'.[60] The challenge is to form communities that facilitate encounter with God and God's people, in such a way that convinces, converts and transforms those who respond to them.

a moment of opportunity and the gift of repentance

Although Western culture will continue to evolve (particularly through technological change) it has taken a shape that it is likely to hold for the foreseeable future. The shape of the mission field has become clear. The missionary task remains the same:

> A changing culture constitutes a call from God. Many people today live in a variety of worlds such as family, job, leisure, politics and education. These worlds represent different social structures.[61]

The gospel must be proclaimed afresh within these different structures. They present a moment of opportunity, a challenge to confidence in the gospel, and a call to imaginative mission.

> So far from foreclosing the possibilities for appropriate Christian living, these conditions actually open the door to new variations, new combinations of authentic and responsible action. The demise of Christendom reduces radically the temptations of power, clearing space for the old story to be retold.[62]

But this is also a moment for repentance. We have allowed our culture and the Church to drift apart, without our noticing. We need the grace of the Spirit for repentance if we are to receive a fresh baptism of the Spirit for witness.

If the decline of the Church is ultimately caused neither by the irrelevance of Jesus, nor by the indifference of the community, but by the Church's failure to respond fast enough to an evolving culture, to a changing spiritual climate, and to the promptings of the Holy Spirit, then that decline can be addressed by the repentance of the Church. For true repentance involves turning around and living in a new way in the future. A diocese or parish, which, out of repentance, grows a new relevance to the contemporary world, may also grow in numbers and strength, because the Spirit of Jesus has been released to do his work.[63]

some questions for discussion

> Is it important for a church to meet on Sunday? What factors influence church attendance in your area and how might your church respond to them? (Bible suggestion: Exodus 20.8-11.)

> Over the past 20 or 30 years, what have been the major changes in way of life for people in the community where you live? What effects have any such changes had on the life of the Church in your area? In what ways has your church responded and what more could be done?

> Make a list of the different geographical groups, people groups and networks operating in your community. Compare this against a list of networks with which your local church is involved. Are there people groups, networks or areas where the church is not involved, but *should* be? What might be done about this?

> This chapter asserts: 'In the future, this approach to life [giving people the sense that they can have whatever they want] will not just apply to consumer goods – it will be applied to all aspects of life.'

In your local church, what experiences do you have of people being 'consumers' of faith and religion only taking the parts that suit them or that they want? How do you feel about such people?

What can the church do to challenge a consumerist approach to life and faith, while also following the good missionary principle of meeting people where they are?

> This chapter ends by saying: 'this is also a moment for repentance. We have allowed our culture and the Church to drift apart, without our noticing'.

On reflection, can you give any examples of church and the contemporary culture drifting apart in your area?

What practical things can be done to reconnect the church and society in your area?

What forms of repentance by the Church might be helpful or appropriate in reaching out to those outside the Church?

the story since *Breaking New Ground*

Since *Breaking New Ground*, new styles and approaches to mission have been developing. In the changing mission context, identified in Chapter 1, new movements by God are evident. Things have been happening, and there is growing understanding of the need for fresh approaches in mission and church planting.

snapshots since 1978

In the late 1970s, church planting in England was largely unknown. The Church of England was familiar with the idea of daughter churches, and in the decade following each world war the century-wide overall decline in opening new church buildings was reversed. A good example of newer starts was the clutch of Area Family Services, begun in local secular venues in a single parish, under two successive incumbents in the town of Chester-le-Street.

Church growth thinking arrived in the UK via the Bible Society in the mid-1970s, sowing ideas that growth – both in quality as well as quantity – could become normal. This growth was understood as developing the work of existing churches, not creating additional ones. This may have assisted the birth of a more outward-looking church, but was not a direct precursor of planting and unhelpfully has often been confused with it.

Only three fresh expressions of church were planted in 1978, and of those one was the reopening of a closed church building. It is not clear why, by 1983, this number of church plants had trebled to nine, or in 1985 fifteen examples were begun.[1] In 1984 the first book on the subject was published for the English market – *How to Plant Churches* – from the British Church Growth Association.[2] It comprised papers from an earlier interdenominational conference, but the essays mixed enthusiasm and caution. The first Church of England church planting conference was at Holy Trinity Brompton, London in 1987.

church planting heydays?

From 1987 to 1991, what began at Holy Trinity Brompton as a gathering of private invitees became an annual open event. It attracted many hundreds of attendees across the traditions: existing plant leaders, would-be explorers and some diocesan permission-givers such as archdeacons. The number of churches planted each year continued to rise, reaching about 40 per year in 1990, a figure sustained until 1992. The 1991 conference papers became the book *Planting New Churches*,[3] which is still the most substantial work from Church of England authors on the subject. There was no lobby or formal network of planters, just expanding friendship groups sharing the vision at every opportunity and level. Within five years an unknown fringe activity had made its way onto the main stage of church thinking and practice.

One observed phenomenon at the time was the proportion of churches planted that crossed parish boundaries. The annual closure rate of church buildings was then in excess of churches begun, and a spate of pastoral reorganization was in progress. From 1985 to 1991, 25 per cent of cases involved a cross-boundary dimension, such as a partnership with an existing weakened church or the reopening of a closed building.

The vast majority were begun with diocesan consent, but of the 370 in the last 25 years, 4 in 1991 took the radical course of proceeding without those permissions. Local 'invaded' incumbents voiced strong disapproval, and media interest emphasized conflict within the Church and the threat to the future of the parochial system. These factors led to the October 1991 House of Bishops Standing Committee to call for the formation of a working party on 'church planting'. Their work became the 1994 report *Breaking New Ground*.[4]

what did *Breaking New Ground* say?

church planting is legitimate

The introductory letter from the Chair, Bishop Patrick Harris, set out a framework:

> The conclusion of the present report is that the structures and Canons of the Church of England are flexible enough to allow bishops to encourage and to enable Church Planting to take place in their dioceses. Where there is goodwill on all sides, new congregations can

be planted even across the boundaries of parishes, deaneries and dioceses.[5]

Despite problems at that time with cross-boundary plants, the 1994 report was positive about church planting as part of being Anglican in mission.

> The working party believes that church planting is not an erosion of the parish principle of mission in the Church of England. It is a supplementary strategy that enhances the essential thrust of the parish principle.[6]

At the time people were unsure whether planting represented opportunity or danger. Thus the word 'supplementary' is worth comment. A Grove booklet commentary on the Report noted:

> Here is tacit admission that church planting is not simply a new option in mission; it has begun to affect Anglican identity and our doctrine of the Church. To 'supplement' is to add something different, or to insert something missing. To add in this way is to change. Planting is not simply creating more of the same churches; it focuses recognition of larger changes in the Church of England and is a response to them.[7]

parish and network are both valid

The first chapter of *Breaking New Ground* marks a shift in thought. Entitled 'Church planting – opportunity or danger?' it reflects the 1991 context. The subtitle, 'A vision of Church: territory, neighbourhood and network', speaks relevantly to today's understanding of an Anglicanism that needs to work with each of these three dimensions. It moves on our thinking without destroying former ways of working, and accepts the need to add to those understandings of the past.

The 1994 report maintains the traditional Anglican value of *territory*, delivered through the parish system. It develops the theme that, in the twentieth century, Anglicanism has been forced to accept the reality of *neighbourhood*. Since the industrial revolution this has not always been physically the same as 'parish', and so the report drew attention to 'population movements . . . [making some parish boundaries] . . . irrelevant anachronisms'.[8]

The third factor at work, *network*, is formed socially and culturally, not by physical area. This, too, is recommended to be part of our national and local mission. Mission seeks to relate to society as it is and to people as they are, rather than expecting people to conform themselves to 'our' way of operating or structuring our church life. At one stage *Breaking New Ground* concludes:

> Many in the Church of England, and not just those involved in church planting, are asking for recognition that human life is lived in a complex array of networks and that the neighbourhoods, where people reside, may hold only a very minor loyalty.[9]

As the established Church, the Church of England has a special responsibility to seek to be a Church for the nation. We are to serve those who reside in the geographical area of each parish, care for those who live in neighbourhoods that may overlap with parish geography, and minister to those who inhabit networks that are disconnected from the notion of parish or territory. Each is equally our responsibility and our care.

stories and guidance

Breaking New Ground contained stories of positive and less positive ways of church planting. It offered definitions of 'church' and 'plant'. It gave guidelines and advice, but avoided formal constitutions and tight procedures that might crush vitality or zeal. And it included steps on how, in partnership with the diocese, to mature a church plant.

As a report, it was primarily permission-giving, not future-looking. General Synod debated the report and commended it for study to the wider Church.

life moves on

Since 1994, experience has taught a variety of lessons.

from cross-boundary to non-boundary

Breaking New Ground was written partly as a response to concern about cross-boundary plants. Cross-boundary plants have diminished from 25 per cent in 1985–91, to 17 per cent since 1992.[10] A decline in the closure of church buildings has meant that there are fewer redundant buildings to adopt, and the two- to three-year negotiations involved in crossing a parish boundary may also be daunting. However, with new house building set to increase up to the year 2020, the percentage may go up again.

In a network-based society there is a shift towards the planting of 'non-boundary', network churches. Over a dozen (mainly urban) have begun since 1995. They have developed as a mission response to particular cultures and groupings that are not reached by existing churches. (Further comment and examples are given in Chapter 4 of this report.)

an explosion of diversity

There were hopes in the early 1990s that church planting would continue to increase in quantity, but the reality has been an increase in diversity. Many different strands of church planting and other ways to explore being church arose in the 1990s. Chapter 4 will examine their dynamics and characteristics.

The sheer variety of fresh expressions of church has been a welcome sign of continued spiritual creativity in the context of a rapidly changing mission climate. Not all fresh expressions of church would themselves use the words 'church' or 'plant'. They also revealed, across an untidy spectrum, some common perspectives around the growing question 'What is church?' Assumptions about forms of worship and community, day of meeting, size of key unit, and the starting point in mission, have all been challenged. Greater flexibility of approach, and the need for principles beneath practice, have been revealed. These insights are explored in Chapter 6.

Within the diversity of fresh expressions, a number of common themes have emerged:

- The Church derives its self-understanding from the *missio dei*, the ongoing mission of God's love to the world.
- The Trinity models diversity as well as unity.
- Creation reveals God's affirmation of diversity.
- Mission to a diverse world legitimately requires a diverse Church.
- Catholicity should not be interpreted as monochrome oneness.
- Election and incarnation reveal God daring to be culturally specific within diverse contexts.[11]

create don't clone

The Anabaptist writer and practitioner, Stuart Murray Williams, has been the most trenchant critic of the tendency of older church plants to copy the outward forms and style of their sending church, without asking whether the new mission context was different. This can result in failure to let the shape and form of the new church be determined by the mission context for which it was intended. The call for new kinds of churches can become subverted into the production of more churches.

The science of genetics helps us understand a difference between creative reproduction and cloning. When the genes of an individual are combined in offspring with new genes from an external source, the result is a genetically unique creation in the next generation and not a copy. So it is with good church planting practice.

> **The planting process is the engagement of church and gospel with a new mission context, and this should determine the fresh expression of church.**

To exclude either the theological essentials or the new mission context is to miss what is necessary for plants to take root and lead to a contextualized church. This will be developed in Chapter 5 of this report.

Looking back, some clone plants began as culturally inappropriate entities and so aged rapidly and took on all the unhelpful attributes of the parent. Some failed to survive and failed to reproduce further. However, despite all these weaknesses, what happened in the history of church planting has been enormously important. Planting produced significant numerical growth (particularly in contrast to the general pattern of decline elsewhere in the Church) and led to considerable mission enthusiasm and creative initiative. Where the mission context was the same, creating similar church was sometimes appropriate.

starting *and* developing

It became clear that planting a church was no guarantee that it would succeed. It is therefore interesting to ask what helped them mature.

In the heyday of planting, some of the literature offered 'how to' answers, making assumptions that were inflexible about the forms and processes that 'church plants' would take. Easy and convenient solutions tended to encourage a simplistic approach. They often failed to encourage a more costly, slower and localized methodology, in which the fresh expression was allowed to evolve from its mission context.

In addition, some of the advice from this period was directed to the stages leading up to the birth and early months of the life of the planted church. Insufficient attention was given to the skills needed in later life. 'Church planting' in some quarters became synonymous with the birth process only, and did not embrace the growing and maturing of the plant.

However, a more important factor in the way that church planting developed was what was in the minds of church people, and the assumptions they carried about inherited models of church.

maturity matters

In the 15 years of Anglican Church Planting Conferences, seminars on 'maturing church plants' were always well attended. Such issues were the frequent subject of individual consultancy and even specialized additional conferences.

Looking back, there has been a tendency for the life and vitality of fresh expressions of church to be unduly influenced either by the controlling instincts of 'mother' churches, insecurity among incumbents in those churches or by a change of incumbent. Sometimes there was lack of vision in a diocese to see that a planted church could cease to be an 'interesting experiment', or a 'mission project', and be welcomed as a fully-fledged member church of the diocese. The language and image of mother and daughter churches was rejected in favour of sending and sent churches.

death after life

Not everything that was born in the flurry of church planting of the early 1990s survived. Frequent causes of failure included poor planning, leadership issues, inward-looking focus, cultural blindness, part-time leadership and lack of resources.[12]

It is thought that 90 per cent of Anglican church plants still continue, a figure that compares favourably with some other denominations.

thinking moves on

Breaking New Ground, in a climate that sought tidiness, used language with a certain innocent clarity:

> Church planting normally involves the establishing of a new congregation or worship centre and is to be encouraged as an important part of Church Growth.[13]

Virtually every concept in that sentence is now challenged by the variety that has emerged.

With the advent of Cell Church and Base Ecclesial communities (see Chapter 4), the meaning of the word 'congregation' cannot be assumed.

Even to 'congregate' looks increasingly inadequate to convey the deeper dynamics of church. The term 'Christian community' is both more generic and more flexible.

The words 'congregation or worship centre' reveal a particular understanding of what church is, and exhibit a view of church that remains attached to the 'come to us' mission model. It thinks in terms of Sunday, of corporate worship and holy buildings dependent on ordained leaders. All these are now challenged as defining marks of what it is to be church. Furthermore, those expressions of church seeking to connect with people from post-Christian cultures would say that the provision of worship is not the right starting point.[14]

'Establishing' has some triumphalistic and even mechanistic connotations. A more contextually sensitive approach would use words such as 'evolving' or 'beginning'. Furthermore, church planting resists being seen as part of 'Church Growth', with its evangelical associations. A full variety of ecclesiastical traditions have been church planters, and the label 'Church Growth' can suggest church planting is about adding to the number of existing churches, whereas at best it is about multiplying diverse future churches.

what is 'proper' church?

In 1994, another assumption was that 'church plants' might be bridges to bring people back into 'proper' church.

This image of bridge assumes the Church acts like a magnet and all that is necessary is for human beings to be brought near enough to feel its irresistible attraction. It is as though the Church has ignored what most Western people know:

> Since the seventeenth century more and more people have discovered, originally to their surprise, they could ignore God and the Church and yet be none the worse for it.[15]

Magnets are useless at attracting non-ferrous objects, and many churches are not attractive to post-Christian people. Part of the paradigm shift since *Breaking New Ground* is the discovery that fresh expressions of church are not only legitimate expressions of church, but they may be more legitimate because they attend more closely to the mission task, and they are more deeply engaged in the local context, and follow more attentively the pattern of incarnation.

plan or discern?

Breaking New Ground stated that:

> Planting is normally part of long-term diocesan planning in partnership with the deanery concerned . . .[16]

The desire for relational consultation and partnership, beyond the independent activity of single entrepreneurial large churches, is still healthy. However, two other factors have revealed the inadequacy of this strategy:

- It is a rare diocese that has any long-term plan for planting churches with which a mission-minded local church could cooperate.
- Practitioners working at the edge of the Church are more in favour of planting as a response to what has happened when/where the good news in Christ has been sown in a culture, people group or local area. Some prefer to talk of sowing the gospel and seeing what results. The response shapes the form of Christian community. It is more like a process of discerning the prior action of God. As such it is an outcome of the instinct that

> Ecclesiology is a subsection of the doctrine of mission.[17]

Planning for predetermined outcomes is legitimate but no longer primary. A mission-informed response, rather than a structural initiative, is now seen as authentic. Much that now happens is ad hoc and not officially planned – it is 'pre-official'.[18]

wider church developments

diocesan survey

As part of the preparation for this report, the working group initiated a survey of dioceses. The outcomes of that survey helped set the agenda for the shape and content of *Mission-shaped church*.

The survey gave dioceses the opportunity to identify particular issues or areas of concern. There was a general request for guidance on straightforward good practice. Leadership, both local and diocesan, was seen as crucial, along with ongoing training, support and mentoring.

The survey showed that organized record keeping of church plants and fresh expressions of church is sketchy, with a few exceptions. We will recommend that good record keeping is established in each diocese, so that all expressions of church are known and taken seriously, and so that lessons from their existence are identified and applied. In addition, we will recommend that fresh expressions of church and church planting should feature significantly in lay and ordained ministerial education and training.

planting and the experience of denominations

In the early 1990s all denominations and new church streams developed programmes of church planting. Many appointed national officers and prepared training materials and resources.

An interdenominational UK-wide congress on church planting in 1992 grabbed media headlines by announcing enormous future goals. The outcomes fell far short of the hopes and aspirations. A detailed account of what has happened in church planting during the past decade is available from a number of sources, and in particular in a number of denominational reports,[19] and a recent Grove booklet.[20]

post-denominational?

Younger generations are moving from being ecumenical to being post-denominational. Surrounded by secularism, materialism, competing spiritual movements and other world religions, simply being authentic Christians seems sufficient to them. Add to this the mobility of younger generations, and possibilities of real choice about where to affiliate, and denominations per se are not seen as desirable designer labels, only as different types of clothing, most of which are not thought 'cool'.

Breaking New Ground urged ecumenical planting wherever possible. However, Local Ecumenical Partnerships (LEPs) account for only around 9 per cent of Church of England-linked plants since 1967. LEPs are nearly always found connected to new housing on greenfield sites and in New Towns. In these contexts, there is less past baggage, and partnerships may be easier to form. The percentage of plants begun with informal ecumenical cooperation has been higher.

Practical advantages and disadvantages of the LEP plants are summarized in Chapter 7. The main tension is that cooperation seems so sensible, but mechanisms for it are so cumbersome. Further, experience shows that LEP plants seldom, if ever, go on to plant again.

is church planting passé?

After the 1990s' peak of interest in church planting there came a stream of other supposed solutions to mission ineffectiveness: Seeker Services, the Toronto blessing, the Alpha course, Cell church, Celtic Worship, Pensicola Revival and most recently the 'Transforming Communities' videos. Many of these initiatives have been wrongly interpreted as offering a 'quick fix' to the mission dilemma of the Church. Enthusiasm for these new options has perhaps diminished enthusiasm for exploring costly and prayerful ways of enabling church to grow and develop in non-church cultures and places, and church planting has tended to take a back stage position.

In a survey of church planting over the last decade, George Lings and Stuart Murray Williams note a decline in activity in the second half of the 1990s, but then renewed interest since 2000. They conclude:

> There is evidence, however, of increasing planting activity . . . Planting does not have its previous profile, but there are signs of resurgence. In our judgement, the level of activity is higher than five years ago and the pace is quickening.[21]

insights from other parts of the world

contributions from other parts of the UK

A notable recent contribution in this field is the Presbyterian Church of Scotland's report *A Church without Walls*.[22] It gives excellent summaries of the changes in mission climate they face; the contours and processes of emerging church as they envisage it; an honest list of the inhibiting factors in existing church life to overcome; and proposals for continuing reform.

The Evangelism Research Group of the Church in Wales' Board of Mission produced a document of similar significance, *Good News in Wales*.[23] It describes by story and analyses the variety of other responses that have emerged, and highlights a call to let mission shape ensuing ministry patterns. Archbishop Rowan Williams wrote the foreword.

> We may discern signs of hope. These may be found particularly in the development of a mixed economy of Church life . . . there are ways of being church alongside the inherited parochial pattern.[24]

Both reports are accessible to most local church leaderships and make good study or discussion volumes. They make excellent companions to this report.

contributions from the worldwide Church

The sources, insights and comments from the world Church are wide. If we ask, what might the 'world Church' contribute to new ways of being church in England, we can see that:

- It offers the opportunity of widening our awareness, expanding our imagination and vision.

- It offers the resources of people: Christians from other countries who come to England and those Christians encountered by people from England going abroad. This cross-cultural experience and encounter can both challenge and change us.

- It offers different ways of doing things. Those ways may not directly transplant into English culture and context, but they may be adapted or provide spin-offs that fit our situation better.

- The 'world Church' can open our eyes to traditions within our own history that have disappeared or gone underground.

- Many Anglican mission agencies now provide a substantial resource for the missionary church in England.

- Finally, the witness of the world Church is constantly flowing into the Church of England from our international connections. Perhaps there can be a more intentional, more open humility to reflect on that influence and what can be learned and applied practically from it.

conclusion

Breaking New Ground exemplified its time and context. It encouraged containment, safety and gradual development within the existing legal framework, and it helped legitimize church planting. But the 'how to' question that was fundamental to *Breaking New Ground* is being rapidly overtaken by a more radical question – 'why to'. There are now fewer books on church planting practice, and many more reflect radically on what church is and think creatively about it. In response to the changes of the world and the crisis of the Church there is an increasing interest in exploring 'what is church, and what is church for?'

some questions for discussion

➤ Do we need more and different churches, or simply better existing churches, or both? (Bible suggestion: 1 Corinthians 3.10-16.)

➤ All churches were once church plants of one sort or another – a new initiative designed to connect the gospel with different people and/or in a different way. How and why was your local church started?

➤ What to you are the *essentials* that are needed for a Christian group or fellowship to be recognized as a proper church? What other things could be risked or compromised to allow the gospel to flourish?

➤ This chapter observes that: 'it is a rare diocese that has any long-term plan for planting churches'. How much do you know about your diocesan strategies for mission and growth and how have these impacted on your church? How might your local input help the diocese to encourage church planting and fresh expressions of church?

➤ This chapter says: 'mission to a diverse world legitimately requires a diverse Church'. Can the Church ever become *too* diverse? How might your own local church diversify in order to meet different needs? What kinds of resources are necessary for such diversity and how could you obtain them?

chapter 3

what is church planting and why does it matter?

As early as 1991 Revd Bob Hopkins, the convenor of the Anglican Church Planting Conferences and author of two Grove Booklets[1] on the topic, coined a working definition.

> Church Planting is creating new communities of Christian faith as part of the Mission of God, to express his Kingdom in every geographic and cultural context.

This concise wording has stood the test of time. It is theologically well-connected, flexible about forms of church and the varieties of mission task.

'Church' and 'plant' both have a variety of meanings. But when the two are combined, they modify each other. *Breaking New Ground* rightly argued that the two words, 'church' and 'plant', should be used separately and not used as a new hybrid noun – a 'churchplant'. It is important that what comes to birth is recognized as church and the verb 'plant' is allowed to indicate an organic process.

what is church planting?

Breaking New Ground paragraph 2.2 thought in terms of 'the transposition of a worshipping community of people into a located place or building'. It described the usual characteristics of a church plant as follows:

- It arises from a conscious evangelistic purpose to inaugurate a congregation.
- It involves the transfer of people from an initial congregation to create or revitalize another congregation.
- It has a known corporate identity and style.
- It has an identified leadership recognized by others inside and outside the plant.
- It has identifiable pastoral structures.
- It is intended to serve an identifiable group, culture or neighbourhood.[2]

a sharpened understanding of the process

This list is still useful. The last characteristic affirms that planting is best done intentionally, with a particular context in mind. The discovery since then has been that church planting that sets out to serve an 'identifiable group, culture or neighbourhood' cannot begin with a clear understanding of what form or expression the resultant church may take. A New Testament analogy, from 1 Corinthians (used there for another purpose) reflects what is now known about all planting:

> When you sow, you do not plant the body that will be, but just a seed . . . But God gives it a body as he has determined.[3]

The experience of best practice in planting since 1994 has been that the previous verse in 1 Corinthians 15 is equally relevant – 'what you sow does not come to life unless it dies'. This echoes Jesus' own teaching on the significance of his own death (John 12.23ff). Jesus presents a picture of seeds dying ultimately to enable creation of further seeds. Planting inherently involves movement and change. Seeds must be taken out of the packet and placed in the soil of the mission context, where the seed itself (in this context the planting team) dies to its original life. The seed loses its previous identity, which was to be part of the sending church with its particular manifestation and culture. It will become something different from what it was before. Dying to live is inherent in the planting process.

Breaking New Ground used language of 'transposition' and 'transfer'. The first was better, for it implied some internal change, as well as external relocation. 'Transfer' only carries ideas of the latter. But neither word does justice to the radical change involved. The planting team (or seed), by mixing with its context, becomes rooted there and draws nourishment and resources from that environment. By this process it dies as a seed, changing from what it was. It becomes a new body of believers, as well as, hopefully, a body of new believers.

The planting analogy has real strengths, for it conveys idiomatically what should occur theologically in all cross-cultural mission. In the UK of the twenty-first century it may be fair to comment that everything we face in mission is now a cross-cultural task. It is not implied here that all old churches must die and that only new ones have a right to live. Churches of whatever age, when they embark on planting, will find themselves confronted by the dynamic of dying to live.

The remaining characteristics of the above list are more to do with the features that a planted fresh expression of church will need to exhibit.

Within the analogy of seeds and plants, perhaps these factors are a list of the basic genetic factors that must be in the seed that is planted, for then they will become expressed naturally in the body that results. The list includes communal identity, supported by local leadership and relationship with the wider Church, as well as practical structures of ongoing care. The list ought now also to include reference to Christ, worship and discipleship, in order to be more fully rounded and specifically Christian. The final characteristic can act as a helpful reminder that this young church, which was planted, is intended to remain apostolic and missionary, even when it has survived its birth and infancy. Mission should never go off the agenda, because it is part of the basic genetic material and impetus for the life of the Church.

the use of the word 'planting'

Words tend to acquire a history and among some people 'planting' has acquired a mixed reputation. When the process is unthinking cloning, or when it is aggressive, or when it involves transplanting large groups without attention to the mission context or other existing churches, then it will deservedly gather a bad name.

But the word 'planting' is still useful. Other phrases have developed in an attempt to describe the variety of different types or styles of church that are arising. Phrases such as 'new forms of church', 'new ways of church', 'new expressions of church' all have some value, but they tend only to refer to 'church' and ignore the process and mission energy through which these new ventures come into existence.[4] These phrases also fail to distinguish between changes to an existing church (such as a church that decides that it wishes to become cell-based) and the processes that mark the creation of a new church.

This report hopes the wider Church may come to recognize what planting is. For example, mergers of struggling churches, or acquiring new buildings, are not church plants. Invasions by church congregations that do not engage with, or become changed by, their new context are probably not planted churches – they are church takeovers.

the difference between process and consequence

Church planting is best thought of as a verb. Until the mid-1990s what resulted from church planting were called 'church plants', and were treated as nouns. Today there is some uncertainty about whether this use of language and terminology applies to the whole range of fresh expressions of church.

Church planting is a process. It is a branch of practical mission theology, developing the thinking and disciplines that underlie the creation of fresh expressions of church. The variety of fresh expressions is the fruit of the planting process. So, in Chapter 4, the term 'traditional church plant' has been coined to describe just one strand of fresh expressions of church – a subset of the planting phenomenon and process.

This report suggests the following as a definition of church planting.

> **Church planting is the process by which a seed of the life and message of Jesus embodied by a community of Christians is immersed for mission reasons in a particular cultural or geographic context.**
>
> **The intended consequence is that it roots there, coming to life as a new indigenous body of Christian disciples well suited to continue in mission.**

what is 'church' in the planting context?

Breaking New Ground examined 'church' in the specific context of church planting. It is a useful starting point.

> Church . . . has been defined for the purposes of this report as: a group of Christians predominantly drawn from a discernible neighbourhood, culture or network who are led by those with authorization from the wider Church, whose worship and common life includes regular commitment to preaching the Word and to the celebration of the two dominical sacraments.[5]

much to affirm

Church is here seen as people more than buildings. It has a sense of rootedness, and is intentionally part of a place – whether the church of Colossae or Colchester. Rootedness embraces culture and network, as well as just location and territory. It includes a connection to the wider Church that involves accountability. Worship and common life are two of its characteristic features. Word and sacrament are balanced and explicitly included.

however . . .

Hindsight exposes some weaknesses in the *Breaking New Ground* understanding of 'church'. The vast majority of that report describes what church *does*, but it is weak on the nature, design and purpose of church. It was a functional description of what a 'church plant' needed to do in order to establish itself, and lacked reference to mission identity or practice. All too often this functional approach to church planting – 'this is what you do' – has led to the planting of non-missionary churches that unsurprisingly have failed to thrive.

> **Planting is a process, but unless and until the kingdom and the mission are in the DNA of the seed of the church, what is planted will prove to be sterile. If mission is not located within the identity of church, planting is very unlikely to recover it.**

words to describe varieties of 'new' church

A number of phrases have been coined since the early 1990s as a way of describing 'new' types or styles of church. These include:

- **New forms of church**, a phrase that suggests that the inner essence of church does not change – it is only the external face that alters.

- **New ways of being church** is more radical language. It considers that the word *ekklesia* has been wrongly interpreted to mean simply 'congregation', so that attendance has replaced discipleship, membership has replaced community, and internal functions have been prioritized over both evangelism and social involvement. Those using this phrase are suggesting that church should be an embodiment of the patterns and priorities of the New Testament, lived out in our mission context.

- **Emerging church** stems back to Robert Warren's mid-1990s work *Building Missionary Congregations*[6] and *Being Human, Being Church*.[7] Emerging suggests an evolutionary, Spirit-led process, and the phrase is a helpful reminder that church needs to emerge from engagement with a context. However, the phrase may invite the existing church to play for time and wait and see what happens, rather than face the urgency of the mission task.

The phrase **fresh expressions of church** is used in this report. The Preface to the Declaration of Assent, which Church of England ministers make at their licensing, states 'The Church of England . . . professes the faith uniquely revealed in the Holy Scriptures and set forth in the catholic creeds, which faith the Church is called upon to proclaim afresh in each generation.' The term 'fresh expressions' echoes these words. It suggests something new or enlivened is happening, but also suggests connection to history and the developing story of God's work in the Church. The phrase also embraces two realities: existing churches that are seeking to renew or redirect what they already have, and others who are intentionally sending out planting groups to discover what will emerge when the gospel is immersed in the mission context.

The weakness of the phrase 'fresh expressions' is that it does not easily differentiate between the two realities mentioned above – those who are discovering new life within (which overflows in mission), and those who deliberately go out to immerse church and gospel elsewhere. For this reason this report speaks about both 'planting' and 'expressions', and commends this vocabulary. Both planting and fresh expressions of church can arise out of similar motivation and experiences, and both can overlap in what they seek to achieve. They are different but connected realities, and the Church needs both.

why are church planting and fresh expressions of church important?

Church planting and fresh expressions of church offer important ways forward in mission, both pragmatically and theologically.

being faithful to the Anglican tradition

kingdom is at the core

All churches and denominations are called to be signs of the kingdom of God. Lesslie Newbigin argues they are signs and first fruits, but not to be seen as agents of the kingdom, for that is one role of the Spirit.[8] No one denomination, nor a strand within it, will be sufficient to respond to the call, to provide all the signs, or meet all the needs. The old and new expressions of church and the resources found in them all are needed.

However, Anglicanism has a basis that should especially motivate it to connect with fresh expressions of church and church planting.

to fulfil the Anglican calling

The Church of England exists to be a Church for the nation. This is not a comment on the issue of the Church being established, but a statement of its mission purpose.

The parochial system, which for centuries has been the delivery-system of the conviction of 'Church for the nation', might be compared to a vast slab of Gruyère cheese. Its nature is to present as one solid reality, but examination shows that by its nature there are lots of holes where there is no cheese. In theory everyone has their local church. *Breaking New Ground* identified the reality:

> There is increasing recognition that in many areas of urban England there are pockets of 2000–5000 people who are unchurched for all practical purposes.[9]

The Anglican calling, because of theological conviction, is to be a Church for all. Church planting and fresh expressions of church can help to identify and begin to fill the geographical and cultural gaps. They also represent ways to engage with the cultural and network patterns within which people live their lives. To be a Church for the nation, the holes in our national network need to be filled. To be Anglican is to want to be rooted in communities and to be accessible to those communities (however those communities define themselves).

to affirm Anglican diversity

An important feature of Anglicanism is its comprehensiveness. The Anglican Church is committed to diversity, held by a sense of unity that transcends narrow claims to truth. In addition, a feature of Anglicanism is that it is found among all kinds of people. Diversity is part of our strength in mission. But at a local level this commitment to diversity and accessibility to a wide range of people faces difficulties. How can diversity and accessibility be sustained through one style of ministry and worship, in a single congregation or single church parish? A combination of clergy and congregation that is simultaneously Catholic, Liberal, Evangelical, Broad and Charismatic does not exist. Further, this impossible combination is simply a selection of ecclesiastical styles and interests – it does not include the wide variety of personalities, cultures and experiences found within non-church society.

Diverse, principled, sensitive church planting and fresh expressions of church are one way in which the Church of England can further our characteristic and desirable Anglican diversity and unity. This is not just to broaden the choices people have within and across parish boundaries. This is also an exploration of the Church being one, yet not being uniform.

continuing Anglican history

In one sense all Anglicans worship at a planted church. Celebrations of church centenaries and tri-centenaries are an acknowledgement that every church had a beginning. Anglican history is the outworking of the Church's belief that this country is its mission field and pastoral responsibility. Being catholic and reformed, the Church holds together instincts for continuity and development.[10]

rediscover a forgotten dimension

Many models of 'the Church' exist. Some church planters, who reflect on Scripture and tradition in the light of their experience, want to affirm an important dimension that should be fundamental to the Anglican understanding of church: 'The Church is a community with a divine mandate to reproduce.'[11]

Church planting serves as a strong reminder that the Church is called to be essentially, not incidentally, missionary in character. The Church is to be so outgoing that it will reproduce itself, by the Spirit, in all the variety of expressions needed. This direction is at one with the Lambeth 1988 Resolution 44:

> This conference calls for a shift to a dynamic missionary emphasis, going beyond care and nurture to proclamation and service; and therefore accepts the challenge this presents to diocesan and local church structures and patterns of worship and ministry, and looks to God for a fresh movement of the Spirit; in prayer, outgoing love and evangelism in obedience to our Lord's command.

reviewing the mission task in England

Philip Richter and Leslie Francis, in *Gone but not Forgotten*[12], give a sketch, by implication, of different groups in English society, a snapshot from October 1996. Their particular interest in the book centres on researched numbers of those who have left the Church. The diagram very roughly illustrates the proportions involved.[13] This simple diagram is not attempting to take account of the church involvement or non-involvement of people who are members of other world faiths and traditions (6 per cent of the population in the 2001 Census).

Current (or previous) church attendance or involvement

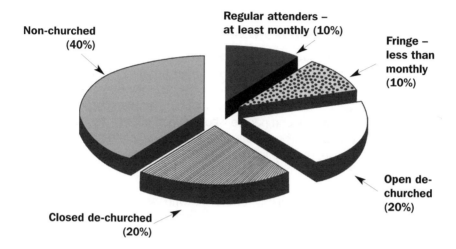

Based on Philip Richter and Leslie Francis, *Gone but not Forgotten*, Darton, Longman and Todd, 1998.

- **Regular attenders**
  Across the denominational spectrum, roughly 10 per cent of the population attend perhaps 5–8 times in a two-month period.

- **Fringe attenders**
  Roughly 10 per cent of the population may attend church 1–3 times in a two-month period.

- **Open de-churched**
  Forty per cent of the population are 'de-churched'. At some point in their life they attended church. Of these, 20 per cent are the 'open de-churched' – people who have left church at some point, but are open to return if suitably contacted and invited.

- **Closed de-churched**
  Twenty per cent of the population have attended church at some point in their life, but were damaged or disillusioned, and have no intention of returning.

- **Non-churched**
  Forty per cent of the population nationally have never been to church, except perhaps for the funeral or wedding of a friend or relation.

This 40 per cent is the national average. In urban areas this figure might be as high as 80 per cent of the total.

what are the open de-churched like?

This group includes those sometimes called the 'lapsed'. They may have dropped out of attending after a house move, or because of a change of vicar, or when work patterns changed or increased. Their non-attendance often began as accidental, through a change in the pattern of their life. Richter and Francis also found people who dropped out of attending for lack of people their own age, difficulty because they perceived the church would censure their lifestyle, realization that the local church could not cater for their children, or the church demanding money.[14]

Further out among this group might be those who went to Sunday school or a youth group; they were married in church, or they are among the 24 per cent who had a child baptized. They would at least consider going to church at Christmas and hope to survive the experience. Yet further out are the people whose parents had those rite of passage links, and those with pressures from the extended family to seek baptism of a child. All these groups are those who sometimes come back to faith, or who find a substance where previously there was only the shadow, through today's forms of relational evangelism and pastoral care. In many cases someone in the family or friendship group has been praying for them – perhaps for years. They come back, which is what church is hoping for. But they are only a minority – just under 20 per cent – not the majority of the population.

what happened to the closed de-churched?

Richter and Francis found that people in this group had had a significant link with a church in the past. Reasons for their departure were varied, but included a sense of boredom and lack of relevance, a sense of rejection when refused the occasional offices, personality clashes and relationship breakdown with church leaders, change of clergy, or disagreement over decisions. Also in this group were those who felt they could no longer attend because they sensed a lack of acceptance, perhaps related to a marriage difficulty or lapse, birth of an illegitimate child, admission of sexual orientation, a divorce, or some form of addiction. Others had left because of what seemed to them a church culture of guilt, control or impossible expectations. Additionally, leavers speak of loss of faith in the face of scientific claims and other world religions, and radical disenchantment with the Church's hypocrisy, and collusion with materialism and prejudice.[15] For these reasons the closed de-churched (over 20 per cent nationally) are probably one of the most resistant groups in society – they have experienced church, and deliberately chosen to be no longer associated.

The closed and open de-churched have been presented above as rather distinct groups, but clearly there are overlaps and a spectrum of views and attitudes.

who are the 'non-churched'?

This is the increasingly large proportion of society that has no history of church attendance – perhaps for several generations. There may be no one living in their extended family for whom church is part of normal life. No one prays for them by name. George Lings notes that church is for some 'an alien and expensive building that I wouldn't know what to do in; worse it is occupied by people I wouldn't be seen dead with'.[16] As mentioned earlier, in urban areas the proportion of non-churched is likely to be much higher than 40 per cent.

This difference between de-churched and non-churched is important. The de-churched have had some exposure to the Church and its message, and they may now be left with favourable or unfavourable feelings about that experience. But the non-churched have no connection with church, nor any real idea what it is about.

Thus it must be accepted that any approach at evangelism or community involvement that assumes we can 'bring people back to the church' can only – at best – be effective for a diminishing proportion of the population. For most people, 'church' is either an utterly foreign culture, or one that they have decided to reject. For the Church in England, the stark reality of this situation should be a cause for profound repentance and renewed missionary endeavour.

they are no longer 'our people'

The Anglican pattern of ministry, built around parish and neighbourhood, can lead to a way of thinking that assumes that all people – whether attending or not attending – are basically 'our people'. All people are God's people, but it is an illusion to assume that somehow the population of England is simply waiting for the right invitation before they will come back and join us. The social and mission reality is that the majority of English society is not 'our people' – they haven't been in living memory, nor do they want to be. The reality is that for most people across England the Church as it is is peripheral, obscure, confusing or irrelevant.

different responses are needed

These five groups in the diagram might be considered to be different tribes for a missionary to face. Each needs a different approach. The sober reality is that we do most of our evangelism, and even our church planting, among the 30 per cent nearest to us – the fringe and open de-churched. But the stark question remains: what of our mission to the remaining 60 per cent of the nation?

Any apostolic church that derives its nature from the apostolic (or sending) character of God has no option but to face its mission to the non-churched, even if this is at the cost of finding new ways of being and doing church to exist alongside what we do and are at present.

> **The task is to become church for them, among them and with them, and under the Spirit of God to lead them to become church in their own culture.**

The gap is as wide as any that is experienced by a cross-cultural missionary. It will require a reworking of language and approach, and it is here that both church planting and fresh expressions of church offer real possibilities.

there is also a time bomb

The Church of England has for generations relied on a 'returners' strategy – that young people will one day come back to church, perhaps when they are older and wiser, or perhaps when they have young families of their own. But this optimistic approach is seriously flawed. Sunday school figures for the United Kingdom over the last century reveal the general collapse of connection and engagement with children and young people.

We are becoming a nation of non-churched people in terms of Sunday school contact. Even by the end of the First World War, the majority of children were not in Sunday school. Those who were 10 years old in 1950 are now fast approaching retirement, and of them 70 per cent were not in Sunday school. That means that the majority of even the elderly are non-churched. The Youth Strategy and Children's Strategies of the Archbishops' Council will seek to bring new life to the Church's involvement among children and young people, both through the development of Church schools, and through imaginative approaches to evangelism. These

% child population in Sunday school UK, 1900–2000

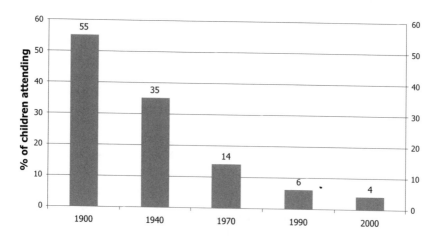

Source: *UK Christian Handbook, Religious Trends No. 2,* 2000/2001[17]

strategies will evolve against the backdrop of very small numbers of children and young people who are currently involved with our churches. Similarly, these initiatives will not touch the majority of the adult population who have had little or no previous connection with church.

The missionary situation faced by the Church has changed. Inviting people back to church as we currently know it may be an effective mission strategy for reaching up to (perhaps) one third of the population who are de-churched. But it is misconceived to assume that this represents a coherent mission approach for the majority of the population for whom church as we know it is peripheral, obscure, confusing or irrelevant.

In this context both fresh expressions of church and church planting offer ways forward. The change is to an outward focus: from a 'come to us' approach to a 'we will go to you' attitude, embodying the gospel where people are, rather than embodying it where we are, and in ways we prefer. Church planting is a helpful reminder that an essential aspect of 'church' is its missionary nature – a fresh movement of the Spirit, in prayer, outgoing love and evangelism in obedience to our Lord's command.[18] Best church planting and most fresh expressions of church reassert the identity of the Church as mission, and both are helping us to rediscover our apostolic identity. If the Church is not missionary, it has denied itself and its calling, for it has departed from the very nature of God.

some questions for discussion

➤ If the Church of England exists for all, then how can it better connect with the many who have little or no discernible involvement or interest? (Bible suggestion: Acts 17.22-31.)

➤ What can be done in your area to enable the non-churched to see and hear the gospel, and to experience Christian life and faith?

➤ What experience have you had of people leaving your church? Can you identify some reasons why they left and any factors that prevented their return? Similarly, have particular factors brought people to join the church?

➤ One section of this chapter says this: 'The Church of England exists to be a Church for the nation. This is not a comment on the issue of the Church being established, but a statement of its mission purpose.' In what way does being the Church of England in your local area influence mission strategy and how does it differ from what other churches and agencies do? Are there disadvantages to being the national church, in your area?

➤ This chapter says there is a 'general collapse of engagement with children and young people'. In what ways does your church already reach out to children and young people and what more might be done to engage them? What further resources would you need for an effective strategy to involve and learn from young people?

chapter 4

fresh expressions of church

This chapter will identify a number of ways in which 'church' is being expressed. It cannot offer an exhaustive list, but simply some examples of key themes and ideas. We expect there will be more expressions and (as we discuss in the next chapter) under God it is right that a variety of ways develop in which different sets of people can connect with Christian community.

Some common features are found in several of the expressions of church that are described here:

- The importance of small groups for discipleship and relational mission.

- These churches do not meet on Sunday morning. This is a response to the large changes in lifestyle in our society over the last 30 years.

- These churches relate to a particular network of people. For example, a workplace church will relate to those who work in that company or organization, and school-based church will use the relationships that are built by people who go to, or whose children go to, the same school.

- These churches are post-denominational. Although the leadership is often part of a denomination, the members may feel themselves to have come from a range of denominations. In churches where the non-churched are coming to faith, then members will typically have a fairly slender denominational identity.

- Some of these churches may have a connection to one or more resourcing networks, including Soul Survivor, Holy Trinity Brompton, New Wine, Reform and St Thomas Crookes in Sheffield. The local church may find it has more in common with churches from outside its area than with other churches in the deanery.

a variety of fresh expressions

What is set out below illustrates the diversity of fresh expressions of church. The list is in alphabetical order. The sections aim to give some snapshot features of each type of expression of church without going into exhaustive detail.

- Alternative worship communities
- Base Ecclesial Communities
- Café church
- Cell church
- Churches arising out of community initiatives (both out of community projects, and the restructuring or refounding of an existing church to serve a community)
- Multiple and midweek congregations
- Network-focused churches (churches connecting with specific networks)
- School-based and school-linked congregations and churches
- Seeker church
- Traditional church plants
- Traditional forms of church inspiring new interest (including new monastic communities)
- Youth congregations.

It is apparent that there is a wide diversity of fresh expressions of church. What may not be so clear is that the depth of information on the different strands varies immensely. Some groupings have already established a track record, grown some level of network between practitioners, thought out their self-understanding and produced resources for internal and external consumption. Other labels used here represent an attempt to group together recent developments that show comparable characteristics, although as yet there may be no network, nor agreed joint understanding and sometimes not even realization that other similar groups exist.

The chapter also suggests categories by which the wider Church may better understand these areas. Insight from these fresh expressions may help existing congregations to reorientate themselves in response to the mission call of God.

alternative worship communities

This fresh expression has been emerging and evolving since the late 1980s. It is a loose grouping that is not always easy to track, partly because many of its adherents have a post-denominational consciousness and a postmodern suspicion of labels and classification.

> This loose network of groups is trying to connect Church, and especially worship, with particular shifting segments of popular culture. In addition they have a passion to close the divide between the experience of

church and the rest of life. They seek to be responsive to post-modern culture, being in touch with preferences for ambiguity and antiquity. They engage with post-modern instincts in the preferences for a multi-media approach. The preferences are to work in a way which is diffuse not focused, created locally rather than remotely, operates contextually rather than institutionally, makes use of the symbolic and the subversive rather than didactic, and is open-ended in style. This represents one of the most thoughtful attempts to relate worship and culture. Thus they have a profoundly mission-based instinct operating behind their worship, though at the same time numbers of groups are distinctly uncomfortable with any aggressive or blatant evangelism, as too modernist, directive and narrow.[1]

The alternative worship (alt.worship) stream, because it is significantly populated by people departing from existing church, contains a strong desire to be different and is among the most vocal in its repudiation of existing church. The firmness of this posture means it is less clear about its own self-identity beyond what it is not, and so far its communities do not seem to have demonstrated long-term stability. It is a cause of major celebration when an alt.worship community lasts ten years.

Alt.worship groups can be criticized for lack of any ongoing engagement with mission – either social involvement or evangelism. However, because they tend to act more as a safety net for those falling out of existing church, they genuinely find it difficult to act as a fishing net for those still outside church. People in recovery from an institution are not the most obvious apologists to invite others to join. As the movement endures there are some signs that this imbalance is being addressed.

A story: Grace in Ealing, London[2]

Grace began in 1993 when a small group decided to put on some services that would be different from the usual at their church. The major motivation was an increasing frustration with a church culture that played music that would never be listened to at home, used language that wouldn't be used anywhere else, and a diet that had become over-familiar and often irrelevant. Church had become something that was 'done to us'. The intention was to seek to worship God in ways and forms that used the cultural resources of the 1990s – the native language of those participating.

One aspect of the Christian tradition that Grace has rediscovered is contemplation. The overall feel of most services is fairly contemplative, and some sort of meditation is usually included. Other features are ritual, discussion, and liturgy that engages people rather than being passively consumed.

Grace is small, experimental and to a degree fragile. Relationships are essential to making it work, and to this end people are encouraged to stay around and chat after services. The team leading Grace is essentially a small group of friends, loose at the edges, without any specific roles or hierarchy except what flows from a person being good at some aspect of something. There is no direct involvement by ordained clergy except by invitation.

Grace does not 'target' visitors but invites them to participate in the worship at whatever level they feel comfortable, recognizing that all are on a journey of faith. The aim is to provide an 'open door' into the presence of God for those who are unfamiliar or uncomfortable with conventional church culture. By being less prescriptive about what people get out of the service, and by allowing the mysterious, ambiguous and allusive, space is made for participants and God to relate on an individual and personal basis. There is room for people who have doubts or questions.

who and what is alternative worship for?

Some stereotypes need major adjustment:

- It is not mainly for youth, despite a universal preference for evenings for worship. Young adults upwards are the typical group.
- It is also quite clearly not an evangelistic attempt at being culturally cool. This is not some form of Seeker Service for the artistic.
- Alternative worship is not an attempt to re-socialize people back into 'real' church. These groups have a remarkably strong sense of community and their own identity. What occurs for those involved *is* church, understood as their place of Christian belonging, believing and behaving.
- Alternative worship groups do not necessarily meet every week and some churches have used occasional alternative worship services as a gentle way of branching out from a more traditional worship style.

George Lings concludes with his wish for them:

> To have confidence in the value of what they do. Their obviously chosen
> task of encultured worship and less trumpeted element of building
> community are both vital. It would help if they were seen by any sending
> churches or parent bodies as a particular kind of church plant, and thus
> encouraged to rejoice in their special identity and to be in healthy
> interdependence with other ways of being church . . . They will need
> to search for ways of mission that are natural to them. Then once more
> they could grow into increasing maturity and continue to be a valuable
> part of the emerging varied missionary movement needed in the Church
> of the West.[3, 4]

Base Ecclesial Communities (BECs)

what's in a name?

Base Ecclesial Communities have their origin in Latin America, and trace
their origins to Brazil in the mid-1950s, although now they are found
worldwide. BECs are strongly identified with people at the bottom or edges
of society, and they offer a gospel of liberation: a church of the poor, for the
poor. BECs work so that people are empowered. They seek to bring hope
and challenge – hope to the oppressed, and challenge that together people
can work for a better society.

Revd David Prior, an English Anglican writer, has travelled the world to
observe BECs. His interest came firstly from dissatisfaction among Western
Christians with existing Church structures.

> Our present structures both deaden and divide, and they also drive away
> many Christians who want and ought to be properly integrated into local
> churches but who find existing patterns of church life stifling and
> unattractive.[5]

The second reason for interest was disillusionment with the house groups
offering a rather trivial agenda – groups meeting the perceived needs of
existing members, rather than existing for the renewal of the Church and
engagement with mission.

Bishop Peter Price is another source of thinking on Base Ecclesial
Communities. In *The Church as Kingdom – a new way of being church*
he wrote:

> The obvious implication of Jesus being with us is to enable us to fulfil
> our vocation in following him – and that we are here to make a
> difference.[6]

Peter Price favours the term 'SCC' – small Christian community – and urges that these must hold together three different strands to hear the authentic voice of God. It involves listening to the daily reality of local life, to the shared life of the small Christian community, and reflection upon both in the light of the Bible. The 'New Way of Being Church' group has evolved a pastoral cycle of five stages: experience, analysis, reflection, action and celebration. Peter Price calls for the widespread birthing of SCCs, a creative interaction between them and the wider parish, and the dynamic use of the Pastoral Cycle.[7]

BECs are widely respected: for the real empowering of people, truly collaborative ministry, practical reflective theological method and use of story. Despite tensions they seek to hold together agendas for radical change with commitment to historic order. At best they know their role is to assist renewal of the church as institution, but it is illusion to imagine they can replace it. Their commitment to radical justice and the priority of the local has led to some nervous central reactions.

BECs have provided an intimate answer to the impersonality of modern existence; a place of faith where everyone can be sure he is accepted and known by name; a group of manageable size, where the pastoral needs of twelve people can be met without stress or ministerial burnout; where a Christian can be fully Church and fully used; where a determined group of twelve working with the Holy Spirit can make a difference in the locality, and in the world at large.[8]

Yet in the UK, outside Roman Catholic practice, SCCs are not that well known. This report had difficulty finding Anglican examples.

A story:
Born out of many years' experience of urban working class ministry, John Summers' conviction grew that there was something missing in the way the good news was being proclaimed among the people of Devonport. The church seemed to be making little progress in terms of offering the gospel, yet Jesus was immediate 'good news' to those he met: the poor, the oppressed, the sick, the 'nobodies'. What was missing?

John Summers' perspective was transformed by a four-day workshop in 1994, led by Fr José Marins from Brazil. Following further workshops at the College of the Ascension in Birmingham, he took his 'learning by doing' back to the churches in Plymouth. There, neighbourhood groups were organized as mission resources, with traditional house groups taking on mission in a wider sense and developing a Jesus kingdom perspective.

The intention here was not to copy Latin American models, but to adapt them to context using common tools and processes. The churches asked the questions: 'What is the Lord saying to us? What does he want us to do? What use is this church in this community and what difference is it making?' It was important to listen to what the local community had to say. One result was that a small sailing yacht, donated to a Plymouth parish, evolved into a staffed programme with a fleet of boats, enriching the lives of disadvantaged young people in the city.[9]

can BECs work here?

- In South America, the shortage of priests and the large number of the poor mean that BECs have been forced to grow up from below. In England the Anglican Church is still structurally present in cities and towns. But the Church of England model of an outside leader, a large imposing building and hierarchical belonging to the wider Church has the effect of alienating many Urban Priority Area (UPA) people, feeding resistance and hindering the growth of indigenous church. In turn, because of the impoverishment of UPA areas, even motivated outsiders find themselves struggling or losing energy. It is hard to begin an upward cycle, when the first step of being an alternative and attractive community that demonstrates the vision through its life and witness is so difficult.

- In South America there exists lay theological and community development training that resources a 'pastoral agent'. S/he helps the BEC reflect in the light of Scripture on their experience, and to coordinate and develop the life of the community. Some are members of religious orders. The lack of pastoral agents in the UK may explain why the BEC model is seldom evident in Anglican churches. It is also true that much English leadership training demands an enculturation into middle class values, which is either alien to, or serves to alienate, leaders from UPA society.

- The institutional church is often concerned about who will pay for buildings and clergy – issues that may be secondary in UPA areas where there is a passion for Christian renewal and direct engagement with God's mission purposes.

café church[10]

This label is an attempt to group examples that seek to engage with café culture and whose external characteristic is a deliberate change of ambience and 'feel' when people meet corporately. In short, gatherings are around small tables rather than in pews. Drinks and often nibbles are routinely available at the start, rather than an option at the end. People characteristically sit and talk, rather than stand or defend their personal space. Interaction rather than spectating is encouraged. The venues are often secular: community centres, youth clubs, cafés and pub rooms. Examples of this expression of church are not yet common.

> ### A story:
> *'Rubik's Cube' is the result of a vision for Bristol churches to reach out to the unchurched within the emerging generation, through meeting, music and making friends. Ruth Hiett, from the 'Rubik's Cube' project, says 'Our "The Rubik's Cube" bar night, every Monday, has continued to grow in both credibility and relationship building. It was rated in a national DJ magazine as being "on the cutting edge of the drum and bass scene".' Further, 'Rubik's Café' night was launched in May 2003 and runs on the first and third Saturday of each month. Ruth describes the café as 'like a magnet' and comments, 'people who have never been to church come regularly to the café and, slowly, they are becoming our friends and becoming interested in our faith'.[11]*

> ### A story: Open House, Brentford, West London, provided by Virginia Luckett
> *The 'Open House Project' is a community café based at St Paul's centre and is part of the parish of Brentford's mission and service to local people. As well as serving delicious food, the project offers prayer ministry, discussion of the Bible and pastoral support through 'listeners'. The café's motto is 'Food for the Body, Food for the Soul' and has a holistic approach, dealing with the whole person, recognizing both spiritual and physical hunger. It provides good food and opportunity to talk, listen, discuss the Bible and pray, so in this way we aim to satisfy both forms of hunger.*
>
> *Open House is based on the 'community ministry' model[12] involving Christians and non-Christians working together, and*

through their common, day-to-day experience of the project
there is opportunity for discussion and the application of
theology to everyday experience. Many regular customers and
volunteers require additional support for their mental health
problems, frailty, physical disability or because they are in
danger of social exclusion. Open House provides natural,
positive opportunities for pastoral care and evangelism.
In a recent survey of customers over half had spoken with
someone about the Christian faith and two-thirds had picked
up Christian literature, wanting to know more.

The Christians involved in Open House see their work as
worship, Christian service and witness through hospitality and
love of neighbour. Several people have come to faith through
their involvement with the project. Open House is still evolving
and is on the edge of new expressions of 'church'. It is an
exciting and challenging experience.

why use café style?

Café church is different from Seeker Services, because café church is
primarily about creating a sense of community, whereas Seeker Services
are often focused on creating an environment where life issues and
Christian insight can be considered. Café church is a fresh outworking
of a long missionary instinct, cited by Gregory the Great in encouraging
Augustine of Canterbury to find what can be taken in the host culture
without fatal compromise, and transform it into ongoing Christian practice.

how radical is this expression of church?

It is fair to ask how far this is a fresh expression of church. People are
congregating in café church, but the dynamic of that meeting is modified.
The encounter with others is in small groups, around tables with drink and
some food, although this is linked to the experience of being part of a wider
community. Worship tends to be informal, although 'informality' does not
necessarily mean dumbing-down either spiritually or liturgically. The notion
of 'table fellowship' in café church goes back to the ministry of Jesus, and
has the potential to create significant meeting between people, and to
encourage the exploration of life and of the gospel. Some have developed
simply 'table liturgies'.

The mission style of café churches is relational. It narrows the gap between
what is encountered in an Alpha course and what is often negatively
experienced on a Sunday. In Alpha people sit around in groups, and a
sense of participation and response is more easily achieved. Café church

could be a style into which people from Alpha groups or similar evolve, because the leap into a more traditional congregational style would be too big.

Café church has been combined with some strands of alternative worship, some elements of small unit church such as cell, some aspects of Seeker Service thinking, and in particular with network church as its mission base springs from its relational community life.

cell church [13]

> Cell church offers a seven-day a week system [of church] that mobilizes and multiplies every member for discipleship, ministry, leadership and expansion.[14]

Cell church represents a 'two-winged' approach to church that seeks to emphasize both large and small group expressions of Christian community. It affirms the following:

- Cell and celebration (the small meeting and the big meeting) are both viable expressions of church.
- Every cell member has the potential to be involved in ministry.
- Each cell is a building block of church.
- Cell leader support and training are essential.

Each cell meeting has a structure within it that enables the cell leader to be a facilitator-leader. A typical cell meeting could express four church functions: worship, word, community and mission.[15]

This expression of church is part of a wider movement across a number of denominations and also across the world. Common to all cell church thinking is a recovery of the conviction that the small group is truly church. There are a number of models being advocated, the Neighbour/Beckham model being the most popular in the Church of England.[16] Some churches are changing existing congregations to a cell model. Others are planting new churches using cell principles.

Cell and other related fresh expressions of church respond well to a culture in which community and family have been eroded, and also address the missionary need of the non-churched for in-depth discipleship into a previously unexplored faith.

change to cell within existing churches

When existing churches undergo the transition to cell principles they work towards becoming a church made up of small groups. Each of the small groups or cells is in nature and practice a full expression of church. The church-like roles of building community, offering worship, hearing and applying the Word, and engaging with society are normative for each cell. Every cell is functionally more than a study group, a task group or even a care group. It acts as the church in microcosm, including the instinct (shared with church planting) that groups should deliberately seek to multiply (principally through relational evangelism) and reproduce new groups.

The alternative is an intentional halfway house, aiming towards a church with small groups, sometimes called Meta Church.[17] The principal difference between pure cell and Meta Church is that in 'pure cell' the cell is the primary unit of church and everything else serves the life and growth of the cells. In 'Meta Church' the congregation is equally valid, and the two modes of church complement one another's strengths. Meta Church's key insight is that small groups are the ideal context for growing skills in local leaders.

can cell church create a growth mentality?

Revd Paul Simmonds, in a Grove booklet on cell church,[18] observes that the move to cell helps shape and direct growth, but does not create it. Cell church originally came from parts of the worldwide Church where growth and evangelism are natural and unexceptional. Cell church was devised to cope with the attendant growth.[19] Thus it is historically true to say that it was not designed to stimulate growth but to channel and develop it.

cell planting

Cell planting involves establishing a new church around cell church principles. At present two different patterns are emerging.

parallel cell church

One is the creation of a cell-based church alongside an existing church that remains congregationally based. The existing membership has choice about the style or expression of church to which they wish to commit. People are discouraged from hopping from one to another. Those who select cell do so in the knowledge that it is fundamentally built around principles of discipleship and relational evangelism. So far the two resulting parallel churches have always been different expressions connected to one parish, and serving only roughly the same area.[20] A small number of parallel cell churches have a specific youth rather than all-age focus.

A story: St Alkmund's, Derby

St Alkmund's is an Anglican church in the Diocese of Derby. Karen Hamblin is director of Youth and Children's Work. She says:

With hindsight I can identify five major factors that moved us firmly in the direction of Cell:

A desire to see real discipleship and not just consumerism.

A longing to see new young people saved and discipled.

A knowledge that youth had more to give and the need to find the right vehicle.

An urgent desire to stop the loss of youth from the church.

A desire to see prodigals returning.

We implemented Cell in September 1997. We felt that we had found something that might have the answers to some of our frustrations in that it would: build on the relational youth work already established; fly in the face of consumerism; create huge potential for evangelism and discipleship; allow young people's giftings to be used and developed in a safe environment . . . In order to develop all our relationships we divided them into three groups, each with two adult leaders meeting in different rooms in the church. Things improved further when we moved out of the church into people's homes, creating a far more intimate atmosphere.

Small groups meet weekly, in church members' homes on Sunday afternoons and then come together to the evening service. We currently have 6 small groups, 2 female and 4 male. Each has a core attendance of 5–6, with up to 8 on each group's list. Once a month we come together as a youth congregation (called Wired), in order to celebrate small group life; all the small groups contribute to this time and have major input in shaping and leading it.

Each cell has a leader and apprentice leader. This means the group is able to multiply through a combination of evangelism (we hope) and new youth moving in from the younger age group. It also helps us cope with the older youth who leave for university each year. However, it means that we are constantly releasing and training new leaders.

True to Cell church, values form the basis for everything. Our values are:

> *Every member ministry*
> *Every member maturity*
> *Jesus at the centre*
> *Sacrificial love*
> *Multiplication*
> *Community life based around openness and honesty.*

NB this parish considered but decided against becoming an overall cell church.[21]

cell from scratch

The second strand in planting is the starting of a cell-based church, for an area or culture where congregational church life is not the most appropriate model. This approach has been used in urban contexts where the desire is to reach the non-churched. Cell makes it easier to travel light. The baggage of church in these contexts may include hostility to the institution, a sense of alienation from its bookish organizational complexity, uncertainty about entering a holy building and a profound sense of not having a clue of what to do once there. Some stories stress the counter-cultural advantage of cell: it is an example of authentic and attractive community that may not be found within the secular community. Where the non-churched have no contact with the institutional church, nor any interest in being contacted, then perhaps a relational approach is the only one that can bear fruit.

advantages of cell planting include:

- Cell principles help those fresh expressions of church working in areas, or with post-Christian groupings, where middle sized or middle class congregations – and their style – would be culturally foreign.[22]

- By being small and responsive to members, cells can identify with the needs of an area and work with those seeking its regeneration.

- Cell assists the multiplication of indigenous leaders, by a deliberate pattern of ongoing apprentice-style training. Finding and forming these leaders is key to the whole process.

- Cell church can help a number of planted churches break through the small church attendance barrier of about 50 people, by breaking down the unit size and raising the proportion of the church membership engaged in all forms of ministry, including evangelism.

- Cell simplifies and focuses the inner life of all young churches. This makes it possible to sustain energy for outward-looking activities.

A story: Harvest, Margate

Harvest was planted out from Holy Trinity Margate in September 1998. This was five years after a previous church was planted (St Philip's, Northdown Park) in the classic mode, which had a new building and a geographical area to serve. Harvest had neither, but was conceived as a network, cell-based, Alpha-style plant.

Careful brokering was needed. The idea was new. No one knew how it would quite work and relate to neighbouring geographical parishes. Fifty-two adults formed the planting core. They met together in six cell groups across the Deanery of Thanet. The cells meet together as congregation on Sunday mornings in a primary school.

Alpha remains the key entry point for Harvest. Members are encouraged to build friendships that enable exploration of the journey to faith. Cells hold regular social events, in homes, pubs or wherever. Seventy-one people have joined since the start of Harvest. Forty-six have moved away. Every cell has multiplied. Some have closed. Harvest is still learning!

can leaders be reproduced?
Cells, and especially those in areas of social deprivation, have to face the challenge of growing the next generation of leaders. Apprentice training can release gifts in people so that they can lead small groups with the support of a clear structure. The reproduction of quality leadership is a potential Achilles heel for cell. There is, however, the possibility that a very different style of leader may evolve from this process. Too often the Church cannot find leaders because it will only accept leaders who work in a narrowly defined (middle class, articulate) way.

the claims
One of the claims worldwide is that the outward agenda of cells, together with a high internal level of intentional discipleship, is what enables cell-based churches to keep growing. By multiplying members and even more importantly creating more leaders through apprenticeship patterns, they claim the ability to avoid hitting a numerical plateau.[23] A few cell churches in Asia have become the largest churches in the world. In the Church of England, perhaps the largest self-styled cell church, led by Clive Collier in Hazlemere, is 800 strong. Some of the largest Church of England churches, though not fully developed cell churches, are vigorously committed to small groups for both discipleship and making new contacts.

'yes, but does it fit here?'
Can cell church really be made to fit with English culture? This question
is relevant both to churches that make the transition to cell, and to fresh
expressions of church. In particular, two cultural questions are asked.

In south-east Asia a highly directive style of leadership is normal, with
a robust focus on discipleship and evangelism. This style is rejected by
some English commentators as a negative and unacceptable form of
control.

In addition, cell church emphasizes that the 'cell' is the primary unit of
church. The instincts of Western Christians are to see the congregation as
the primary unit. This problem should not be underestimated. Even those
in favour of cell argue that it is folly for a church to try to shift into cell
thinking without long and painstaking efforts to ensure the existing
congregation has understood the value change involved.[24] The shift to cell
takes much preparation. Some parishes have begun along the path, but
then pulled back, either settling for some cell values or reverting to an
earlier pattern of house groups for study and aspects of pastoral care.

so what?
Significant space has been given here to cell thinking and practice.
The movement is clear that what it advocates is real church, with cell
worship, community and mission, all infused by a Christocentric spirituality
emphasizing discipleship. There is less clarity around issues of sacraments,
ordained leadership and deeper connection to the wider Church beyond
attending area celebrations.[25]

The variety of contexts in which cell has already been shown to work is
intriguing. That people have been able to vary the extent to which they
adopt its structures widens the attraction. It is the case that, of all the
fresh expressions that have been detected, this one has the highest rate
of adoption by the other expressions. Its flexibility and emphasis on core
values rather than structural methods tells us that cell is a significant
development.

churches arising out of community initiatives

Some churches have begun as a result of community initiatives. In most
instances these initiatives have not been an attempt to create church –
church has developed through or out of the initiative. Churches of this sort
are typically found in areas of social deprivation, and among people that
have experienced significant dislocation from existing forms of church.

why did they start?

In urban areas the proportions of the non-churched are highest. Those called to mission in such contexts know that invitations to worship or attendance at church have little impact. Surrounded by situations and people experiencing significant need, the mission response has been to engage with the local community, and allow local people to set the agenda for what can best help rebuild or regenerate that community.[26]

Communities may often identify the problem of disaffected youth and/or of crime as their most obvious problems. In many cases, work with youth has therefore featured in these fresh expressions of church. This may involve schools work, work with excluded teenagers, weekly clubs, play schemes and holiday clubs. Through these and other forms of partnership, levels of trust are built, as well as growing curiosity in the long-term commitment, style and motivation of the church and its people.

Robert Warren offers a picture of church acting in worship, mission and community.[27] Here Christians in mission to the non-churched have prioritized the building of community as the entry point. 'Community' is understood both as partnership in building local community and modelling community through their own lives.

A story: Hirst Wood, West Yorkshire

Hirst Wood is a small council estate tucked out of sight within the prosperous parish of St Peter, Shipley in West Yorkshire. Its young people are all the non-churched. Even among the older adults, the local team guesses only one third would be the de-churched. The non-churched predominate.
This estimate is borne out by a recent survey in nearby Huddersfield, sampling adults of all ages. It noted that 58 per cent of those interviewed classified themselves as never having had contact with church. With such a challenge a very different approach was going to be needed.

In 1992 a new Vicar, Chris Edmondson, was appointed. Even before interview he only saw the edge of Hirst Wood but thought inside himself 'there's got to be something for here'.

1995 saw the birth of a parish vision and mission statement. One element was a church plant for Hirst Wood as a way forward. It was linked to the desire to appoint a community youth worker for the area.

1996 brought a MSE minister,[28] Pat Gratton, onto the estate.

> On holiday a church friend made a throwaway comment to the vicar about leasing a small property, called Unit 8, on the Hirst Wood industrial estate. In record time the PCC resolved to lease it for five years and completed the deal in December.
>
> 1997 marked the interview of the worker Tim Sudworth. He and his wife Nicki moved in and started work in April. By June Unit 8 had been refurbished by self-help teams, aided by local children who were intrigued by what was going on, was opened by the local MP and began to function. Over the years it has evolved children's and youth work, a club for senior citizens and a midweek chance to learn and pray.
>
> This continuing work has since been renamed 'The Source'.

Sometimes, as in the example above, there has been a clear intention to plant a church through community initiatives. Sometimes the creation of a church has been a 'spin-off', and has surprised the group engaged in the community programmes.[29]

what is the significance of the community initiative approach?

An increasing proportion of the population is non-churched, and in that context what has been discovered here is of increasing strategic importance. These approaches see 'community', not worship, as the key dynamic of being church. People involved are deeply committed to mission, and their actions *are* good news, as well as prompting opportunities to *share* good news.[30]

multiple and midweek congregations

The strategy of working with multiple congregations has a long history. Holding 8.00 a.m. BCP Communion in addition to other Sunday services is probably the best-known example. The monthly Family Service may be another. The intention is to offer different liturgical and communal styles so that different cultural or sociological groups are nourished and sustained within the same building.

In addition to different congregations using the same building on a Sunday, there is also a growing interest in providing midweek church. In the most recent English Church Census, *The Tide Is Running Out*,[31] 51 per cent of responding Anglican churches were shown to offer a midweek service. Those in the Anglo-Catholic tradition are the most prolific providers of midweek worship: 78 per cent of them had a midweek service, compared to 30–50 per cent among other traditions. The value and mission potential of midweek services has been explored in a Springboard and Archbishops' Council resource, *Vital Statistics*.[32]

This sort of pattern of church life appears to be normal and typically Anglican – not a 'fresh expression of church'. But midweek and other Sunday expressions have wider implications and merit careful examination.

- In *The Tide is Running Out*, Peter Brierley reported on youth services:[33] 14 per cent of his church respondents held a youth service, with average attendance of 43.

- The provision of early morning, lunchtime and after-work services for teaching, apologetics and evangelism to the business community is valuable. For some Christians in high-powered travelling jobs, these may be more meaningful expressions of church than their home base versions. The latter often fail to connect with their workplace agenda. They also unintentionally exclude the bringing of friends, because network life means those who work together may live many miles apart.

A story: Welwyn Garden City

At the town centre church of St Francis of Assisi, Welwyn Garden City, there is a thriving Sunday congregation. However, there is also a growing Wednesday congregation. The midweek congregation is composed mainly of women who want to come to church but who also want to give value to family time that is now squeezed into Sundays. If it is not sports events, then other family leisure activities make demands on the amount of time available at the weekend. The Wednesday service includes a sermon or talk, with opportunity for discussion over coffee afterwards. It is timed to follow the pram service in order to encourage parents to stay on from that if they want to.

- Another slowly growing pattern of non-Sunday church is where whole groups have come to faith via an Alpha course, but find the jump from there to congregational worship almost impossible. The style, venue and time of a traditional Sunday service can all be problematic. The best way to help them grow into mature disciples is to begin a congregation or cell that is closer to Alpha in style and feel, and which meets on the same day and time as the Alpha course.[34]

- One common strand here is that midweek church is proper church. People attending don't, won't, or can't attend on a Sunday. The midweek group is their ecclesial community. This will also be true for people attending traditional midweek Eucharists. Increasingly clergy are accepting this situation, and are learning not to regret it, but to build upon it.

A story [35]

A priest inherited a Wednesday morning Eucharist, drawing only ten people. However, it began to grow, and some of those attending never came on Sunday. The priest confronted his prejudices:

'While I was fighting a rearguard action to keep Sunday special, the Holy Spirit had danced ahead of me and was blessing Wednesday. Here, without my properly realizing it, was a church plant . . . that not only provided a place for a new worshipping community to develop, but also had within it people who felt so comfortable and nourished . . . that they were getting on with evangelizing their networks and bringing people to faith.'

Having realized where the Spirit was at work, he put more resources into preaching, some singing and providing refreshments. Once a month they went to the vicarage for a nurturing house group. By the time he moved on, the original ten attenders had become 30, a third of whom never came on Sunday.

new Sunday multiple congregations

The idea of multiple congregations on a Sunday has been rejuvenated in the last few years. Churches that are no longer able to fit their growing congregations into one service have explored this route, as have those who deliberately want to widen the variety of worship that is offered, in order to connect with a more diverse range of people.[36] These are attempts to establish multiple congregations, not simply multiple services. Multiple congregations are where the same building is used at different times on Sunday (or on different days of the week) by separate groups, who are part of the one church in that place, but who function for worship, support, leadership and mission as distinct congregations.

church planting understanding can help

Whether a multiple or midweek meeting is 'church' depends in part on how those who go to it view it. Do the people who attend consider it to be their main way of going to and being church? If people who attend see that time and day as 'their church', then this creates a distinction from a pattern where there are various services on offer, and people choose which they attend on the basis of the type of service, or how their plans are working out for that day.

Churches can enhance the sense of identity within their different congregations by considering some of the following dynamics. The more these are in place, the stronger and healthier will be the sense that each congregation is a 'church' in itself:

- Establish a planned and consistent divergence of worship style – for example an afternoon Taizé congregation, or a service for parents and toddlers, or strongly choir-led worship.
- Grow a dedicated and recognized leadership for each.
- Establish a particular mission focus for the differing congregations. This might be an age-related focus, or geographical responsibility within a large parish, or by concern for a local social issue.
- Provide discrete pastoral care structures for each congregation, which are known by them.
- Deny and refuse all language that calls one of the congregations 'the main congregation'.
- Create an overall team or group ministry in which each congregation has fair representation.

One danger of a multiple congregation approach is that it is often heavily influenced by the worship needs of those who already come. Care must be taken to adopt a clear missionary approach, and seek to connect with a community outside the church, instead of simply using a multiple congregation approach as a way of trying to keep existing church members happy.

network-focused churches

The word 'network' has already peppered previous chapters. Network is a major social reality. Many people still think and live geographically – they may, for example, relate almost entirely to the village or estate in which they live. But increasingly people's lives are best described by the networks to which they relate, rather than simply by the place where they live. Many connect most closely with people where they work or with whom they are at leisure (or even at church), rather than with the people who happen to live nearby. An increasingly mobile society means that the place where people live is decreasingly of importance for them – the important parts of their lives, and important friendships and experiences, are elsewhere.

In 1994, *Breaking New Ground* noted the validity and importance of a church in mission working with networks as well as with parish. The mission opportunity is to connect church and gospel with the culture and way people are living, rather than assume connection will always be most fruitful through locality and parish. An Anglican network church is defined, neither by its Sunday style, nor its philosophy of ministry such as Cell or Seeker, but by whom it is for – people who live in a network environment. The word 'parish' is used in a similar way, to describe who church is for. 'Parish' does not mean a particular theological tradition, nor a type of social setting such as urban or rural. It is shorthand for a church that seeks to serve everyone within a particular geographical area.

Many Anglican churches are consciously or unconsciously serving a congregation of people with a similarity of interest, personality or background. They typically rely on a 'come and join us' approach: if you like who we are, you will feel welcome and at home here. 'Network church' encourages a 'go and inhabit' approach: gospel and church becoming a reality among the variety of ways people are living. They involve not so much cross-boundary as non-boundary church planting, because many people are no longer defining themselves by geographical boundaries. Although network churches are a departure from the classic parish model, they nevertheless represent a valid and Anglican way of fulfilling our national calling to be a Church for all people.

how do these network churches form?

Network churches are developed for mission to particular social and cultural groups. They are shaped by engagement with that particular context and culture, as well as by engagement with the essentials of gospel and the traditions of the Church. Bishop Michael Nazir-Ali argues for this two-stranded method to create all shapes of the Church to come.[37] Some examples of networks are those formed by common work, leisure interest, music preference, or disability (such as the deaf community).

Many network churches see their worship as accessible to outsiders, but the enthusiasm of their members and the use of small groups are usually the routes through which people first come into contact with the worship. These churches are committed to being culturally accessible, as well as repudiating some of the ugly or unchristian aspects of modern life. Similarly, they can be counter-cultural in their approach to the wider

Church and its structures – where structures seem to hinder mission, it is likely that those structures will be bypassed.

hallmarks of these 'network churches'
These churches have a number of similarities and overlaps. These similarities include:

- Identifying social gatherings and meeting points in order to develop relationships with people within a chosen cultural network.
- The use of small groups, where a younger generation can experience community, meaning, and significance. Many use the dynamics of 'cell church' without the actual label.[38]
- Mission expressed through relational evangelism and practical acts of service to local communities.
- Personal mentoring and mutual accountability.

> ### A story: B1
>
> *B1 is a fresh expression of church planted with the active cooperation of Birmingham Diocese. It is a network church, hosted in bars and hotels in the Brindley Place and Broad Street area of Birmingham city centre. Its focus is on non- and de-churched twenty- and thirty-year-olds, who are at home in pubs and lounge bars.*
>
> *B1 aims to be postmodern sensitive, with an emphasis on community, space for questioning and use of varied communication media. It is designed as a church where the spiritually interested, who find church to be irrelevant or a turn-off, can easily belong at different levels, and can observe while they work out what they believe. It worships at different times and in different ways during the month, incorporating aspects and insights of Seeker Services and alternative worship.*
>
> *Originally started with a core of 27 adults, it now attracts 55 adults and 23 children, and sows seeds among a much wider fringe of interested people.*

Although there are similarities, there is also considerable variety in the models of church across the list from this chapter and of mission and worship style.

what is at their core?

Just as part of the essence of parish is to be territorial, the essence of 'network' is not so much to be cross-boundary, but to be non-boundary. The heartbeat of these expressions of church is a passion to engage with a specific social or cultural context across a wide area. They interpret their 'cure of souls' in terms of their current members plus the existing and potential contacts of their members in their spheres of relationship within their shared activities and interests.

Most network churches have declined to adopt methods of pastoral or evangelistic ministry that are geographically based. They do not visit door-to-door, or deliver a magazine to an area. They don't seek baptisms, weddings or funerals outside their existing circle. Some have even volunteered codes of conduct that will return Christians attempting to transfer, to their present churches. As such they seek not to trespass on parish, but to be different from it. By diocesan agreement and often legal entity, they have no parish territory for which they are responsible. Their only base is the relationships their members have with others.

Another common feature is that they seek ongoing relationship with the wider Church. Many have steering groups drawn from within and even beyond the diocese. They have chosen to be more directly and closely accountable to the church-catholic than have perhaps most parishes. This may be partly their Anglican desire to express an identity that is equally local and diocesan, working with the synodical and the episcopal.

take note

There are several further factors that are important in the context of this report.

- It is not yet clear how far these congregations are made up of the non-churched who have come to faith. Large proportions are certainly de-churched, but even if that is the case, then this is still an important and serious area of mission.[39]

- We know that one early example of network church failed. This may be because the leaders did not spend enough time clarifying their vision before beginning. A simple focus on 'the unchurched' is too vague a target, especially when coupled with seeking to operate over a wide area. Other network churches have rightly focused more narrowly on specific groups – such as those who frequent pubs in regenerating city centres, or those who have sporting interests in common.

- The team for a network plant may come from a number of different churches. If this is the case, it is important to spend time developing a cohesive team that shares the same vision and values, as lack of focus in this area will cause problems later if it is not addressed. It is very difficult to sustain energy in difficult times if the team does not share the same vision.

resourcing networks

Within the Church of England there are a number of large churches or networks that actively church plant, or serve as a resource for planting, or that provide a model or template for church planting within particular Anglican traditions. These include New Wine, Holy Trinity Brompton, St Thomas Crookes (Sheffield) and Soul Survivor (for youth congregations). These are an important resource for the mission of the Church of England, because they combine much needed vision, resources and entrepreneurial skill. Cultural patterns can be identified that occur in different places (locally, nationally and globally). It is a source of strength to be able to draw on insights and expertise from elsewhere, while also seeking to inculturate the gospel and church within local and networked places and cultures.

It will be essential to develop partnerships in mission between resourcing groups and individual dioceses. This is already evident in Holy Trinity Brompton's work with the Diocese of London, and Soul Survivor's work with the Diocese of Exeter, among others.

A story: St George the Martyr, Queen Square, London

One of the recent church plants of Holy Trinity Brompton has been to St George the Martyr, Queen Square. It is a parish on the edge of Bloomsbury with much poverty, as well as both refugees and young professionals. In spite of sterling work, in recent years the church had declined to small numbers.

This church plant has been characterized by a sense of partnership with the existing locals, a careful getting everyone to feel part of what is happening. Also, the diocese has played a key role through the local bishop and archdeacon, and the generous support of the Diocesan Finance Committee.

With careful arrangements for the early retirement of the vicar, the whole deanery was brought into a consultation process, and came strongly to support what was being planned. Holy Trinity Brompton sent two clergy and about 100 people to the plant.

Two significant successes of the careful negotiations and partnership are that all members of the old congregation are still there and are not only actual members of the resurrected church but are vibrant members of the new congregation. They have been enfolded and incorporated. The other blessing was that in the first six weeks of the much-invigorated worship and mission 50 people who were local joined the 100-plus people who came from Holy Trinity Brompton.

There has been an overflowing of commitment in worship, outreach and teaching. Careful long-term planning and generous partnership liberate from anxiety and distress and show positive results of new life and new ways of being church in the community.

Partnership with the bishop is the key. There is no room for empire building, or sectarian or illegal action. Nor is there room for treating major churches or networks as somehow 'un-Anglican'. Each diocese needs to include partnership with the major resource churches or networks in its area as part of its proactive mission and planting strategy. The resource churches and networks need to combine faithfulness to their vision with a servant role in the mission of the whole Church. Such partnerships also open up the possibility of well-resourced churches offering or enabling ministry in areas of deprivation.

school-based and school-linked congregations and churches

The Dearing Report[40] identified that Church schools are at the centre of the Church's mission to the nation, and connections between school and church show signs of growing. Some Church schools have begun after-school groups that become church. These meet late afternoon midweek, and may or may not be eucharistic.[41] They draw primary school children, parents of both sexes and grandparents. The more accessible style may suit some newer Christians. Partners of believers can also come, and the comment is often made, 'we understand what you're on about'.

A story: Thatcham, West Berkshire
Thatcham is one of the fastest growing towns in the country. The Anglican team identified work with schools as vital to their ministry in the town. It also became clear that there were significant numbers of Christians in the town whose lifestyles made attending Sunday worship difficult.

In 2001 it was decided to work towards beginning a midweek church in the parish. This became a reality after a Church Army Captain, David Scurr, joined the team. Together with the team vicar, Moira Astin, in February 2003 he started a service on Wednesday at 4.00 p.m. in the parish church, called 'The Link'. From the start it aimed to be 'church', hoping in time to get representation on the PCC and to administer the sacraments of baptism and communion.

People were invited for coffee and a tuck shop from 3.30 p.m. and the service ended at 4.30 p.m. After three months about 20 people were regularly attending, of whom about half did not attend any other service in the week.

Another strand is the use of Church schools to start new congregations, which meet on the premises. School-based worship events become 'church' for pupils and parents. This is perhaps easier to develop at primary than at secondary level, by which time teenagers are less keen on parental attendance and also parents are not naturally in and out of the school as is the case at the primary stage.[42]

A story: Appley Bridge, Lancashire

At All Saints Primary, Appley Bridge, in Lancashire, the Revd Ian Dewar has experimented with using the format of Common Worship in collective worship.[43] He says:

The guiding principle behind what we are trying to achieve at All Saints (church and school) is that of liturgical formation. We have begun to establish a pattern of worship which links church and school together. Every Thursday at 9.15 the school meets in the adjacent church for a midweek service, which follows the Common Worship pattern. After this the children return to school and any adults who wish to stay for Holy Communion remain in church. A similar Service of the Word is held in church on the morning of the third Sunday of the month. This pattern is followed for major events in school where a large number of parents and other relatives who may not otherwise be present are in attendance such as end of term services and the leavers' service.

What this has achieved is to make church familiar to parents and children, even if they do not come to worship on a regular basis. The link between school and church also challenges parents who may have preconceived notions about what church liturgy is like.

The third Sunday service has also proved both flexible and portable in that its format has now been extended to other venues, such as a county school and a local pub.

Because children at All Saints are confirmed in year 7, the next stage is to see how candidates develop from primary school experiences and begin to assume some level of responsibility in the life of the church. So far, some have made connections in helping to establish and lead a youth fellowship and others have taken on liturgical roles, such as chalice assistants in church. In this way, we can see that, while church is taking the initiative to connect with children and parents, children and young people are also feeding back their faith and experience into church, so challenge and change through this missionary programme works in both directions.

seeker church

The Seeker approach was founded by Willow Creek Church in Chicago. It attempts to create an experience of worship and teaching in which 'seekers' will feel comfortable. This involves scrutinizing the content of services, so they are accessible and meaningful to people with little background in Christian worship, and make no assumption about the faith commitment of those attending. Similarly, preaching usually explores everyday issues or life themes (rather than being biblical exposition or specific Christian teaching) – and drama, music, creative arts and contemporary media may also be used to enable connection with the theme through a variety of styles and senses. Seeker Services often take place on a Sunday, although in theory they would happen whenever best suited the potential attenders. In Chicago, services of worship and teaching for Christians take place midweek, leaving Sunday free for Seeker-oriented events.

A story: Bracknell Leisure Centre
Easthampstead Baptist Church already had two congregations in 1999, and began to consider the planting of a third congregation. This became Explore, meeting in a local Leisure Centre. Explore aimed to use contemporary arts to communicate the message of Jesus, while also providing a

community to which people can belong. The primary purpose of this church plant has been to introduce people to the love of God, and in particular to connect with people between the ages of 18 and 40 years.

After much discussion and prayer, the church agreed to go ahead with phases 1 and 2 of a new project to begin this congregation. Phase 1 started in January 2001 with a group of twelve meeting together to pray and to develop a set of core values, a mission and a strategy for this new congregation.

Explore has five key values: community, communication, commitment, caring and celebrating. These are expressed through building friendships, a wide range of social events, seeker-targeted events, small groups and commitment.

Explore is still at an early stage in its life. The initial twelve people who began the church plant now number around 30 adults, most of whom are in small groups. There are clear encouragements as people join the church as a result of the strategy.

what happens in the UK?

There are very few examples in the UK where churches are seeking to model the Willow Creek pattern in its entirety. Willow Creek Church began from scratch, and was hence able to 'target' a particular niche of potential attenders, and did not have to sustain either denominational expectations or persuade long-term church members to make a major change to their normal church habits. However, elements of the Willow Creek model and style of worship have had considerable influence in many Anglican churches. The Seeker Service approach of devising worship for casual attenders or for the curious has influenced numbers of churches in the style and content of their guest and all-age services. In addition, they offer a general challenge to ensure that worship is accessible to all, not just those who are committed Christians, or who are accustomed to the liturgy and traditions of the Church. In addition, aspects of the Seeker approach can be seen in some network churches, and in multiple congregations where one of the congregations aims to offer a more open or accessible style of worship.

It is probably true to say that, in England, Seeker church has been effective mainly in restoring the lapsed, not in reaching the non-churched. It is undoubtedly a resource-hungry form of evangelism, and requires constant creativity and high levels of competence. One evaluation and commendation of the Seeker approach suggests that a team of at least 50 people is needed to sustain a regular pattern of seeker events.[44, 45]

is this a 'fresh expression of church'?

Seeker church does not set out to be a new type of church. It is basically an evangelistic strategy to connect the curious and non-committed with worship and with God. That does not make it a type of church, more a different way in to church. More conventional worship, teaching and the sacraments occur at another time in the week or month.

traditional church plants

What characterizes a 'traditional' church plant?

- It is often located within the parish of the sending congregation and retains close links to the sending congregation, but is seen as a separate congregation, not just an additional service.

- It began as a response to the identification of an area, or a social grouping, that the ministry of the sending congregation did not reach. Accidents of geography such as a major road or railway might divide an area, as might the perceived barriers of different types of housing.

- The planting team who plant the new church might be 20 or more people plus children, and would be given time for selection, growth together and preparation for the task ahead. The planting team might be led by the curate or reader.

- Some form of mission audit, or at least the visiting of prospective new members, would precede any public launch of the new plant.

- As part of the preparation, a secular venue, most often a school or community centre, would be identified as a place of meeting.

- Worship style would be modelled on that of the sending church, with a tendency to be more informal at the plant.

- A public meeting, often with a significant speaker, would bring the new church to birth, often with encouraging numbers of fresh faces attending.

- Numerical growth might decline after the launch, but then creep back up so that what had been a starting team of 20, might be 50 or 70 after 4 years.

- Small groups for discipleship and pastoral care would be set up as part of a deliberate lightweight structure.

- Financial operating costs would be covered by the sending church in year one, and ministry costs might reach break-even by year five.

- Depending on how the following issues were handled, the plant might flourish, plateau or wither.

  ○ Finding the next leader after the curate/pioneer left.

  ○ The enthusiasm of the next incumbent.

  ○ Enabling a significant proportion of the congregation to remain in mission mode.

  ○ Handling the weekly struggles of setting up in a rented or shared building.

  ○ Finding the next home when the initial venue was outgrown.

  ○ Gaining an identity and legal status that reflected a growing maturity.[46]

A story: St Nicholas, Cramlington

Having church planting twins is rare, but St Nicholas, Cramlington – a parish of 30,000 in the Diocese of Newcastle – did it in 1993. The story is told through a video, Reach Out, *that was produced locally.*

Cramlington was a nineteenth-century mining village, near Newcastle, with a Norman church. By the 1990s this was the only Anglican worship centre, in the middle of what felt like a growing New Town. The parish was divided into four areas for pastoral care and it was decided to plant into two of them.

St Andrew's Beaconhill was a pioneer church plant for a neighbourhood. Built around the slim mission resource of the four Christians who lived on that estate, it aimed to reach local people who – for a variety of social, cultural and geographic reasons – would not find it natural or easy to attend the parish church. The planted church saw slow but steady growth.

St Peter's Northburn was a progression plant, also for a neighbourhood community. Its foundation was the strength of the sizeable presence of Christians who went to St Nicholas from that estate. An overall team of 45, including children, was lay-led by two gifted lay people.

These different-sized resources and catchment groups grew at different rates and evolved different styles, both using rented secular buildings. Both now comfortably fill their premises.

Traditional church plants went further than daughter churches in terms of having a specific mission purpose, sending a team, not just a curate, possessing an organic identity, a willingness to be in a more accessible building, and intended growth towards interdependency with the sending church.

'Traditional church plants' may well have a growing importance as part of the Church's strategic response to new areas of housing development, particularly in the south-east of England. However, even in those areas of population growth, a variety of responses and expressions of church will be needed. It will not be sufficient simply to build more churches, but instead a variety of inculturated expressions of church will be needed, including some of those listed in this chapter.

replants

Replants are one particular form of traditional church plant. They involve the reopening of a closed church building. Where there is still an existing congregation, the language of 'graft' or 'transplant' is more accurate. Usually they happen in larger urban areas, because this is where closed church buildings often occur.

Replants tend to start because Christians from a sending church have moved to that area of the town or city. Then they find it unrealistic to continue to commute to church, or to expect their local friends and contacts to travel across town to their existing church. Four out of the fifteen Holy Trinity Brompton church plants come into this category. These have been the fruit of negotiation between Holy Trinity and the Diocese of London, linking the mission opportunity of a redundant building with the relocation of Christians as a mission resource to that area. However, there is no reason why a replant might not be in the style of any of the other fresh expressions of church listed. Contextual awareness and response, rather than cloning a style or variety of church, is always the better missionary approach.

traditional forms of church inspiring new interest

There is some evidence of an increase in attendance at cathedral and other churches offering traditional styles of worship. Some retreat centres are experiencing a growing interest in courses offering various patterns of guided retreat. There are a few stories of new congregations based on the use of *The Book of Common Prayer*, as part of a shift to a pattern of multiple congregations.

The rebirth of centuries-old ways of church and of Christian spirituality is a cause for celebration. It also helps to demonstrate the importance of offering the widest possible range of ways through which people can explore and experience Christian community, church and worship – a variety of types or styles of church for a variety of cultures, contexts and individuals. Something does not need to be 'new' in order to connect with today's multifaceted world. People now as always are looking for mystery, beauty, stability and a sense of God's presence. For some this will be most easily found in contemporary styles and approaches. For others this will be discovered in forms and styles that reflect more strongly the Church's heritage in liturgy and spirituality, and a sense of sacred stability in a fast-changing world.

Fresh and traditional expressions of church should each question themselves about the missionary quality and nature of their community, of their worship and of their purpose. It is possible for any expression of church – new or old – to be inspiring and pleasing, but also too comfortable or unconnected with the mission heart of God. New and old expressions of church need to demonstrate the hallmark characteristics of missionary church that are identified at the start of this chapter.

a new monastic?

'New monasticism' is a category that incorporates a variety of movements, groups and enthusiasms. Most expressions of 'new monasticism' have a dispersed community, rather than being gathered or enclosed. Some, such as Iona or Taizé, have the equivalent of a 'mother house', although those influenced by the spirituality of those communities may never have visited the main community, nor be in any form of organized relationship with them. Other expressions of dispersed community include the growth of Tertiary Franciscans, the slow growth since the mid-1970s of the Northumbria Community, and the recently launched Order of Mission, based from St Thomas Crookes in Sheffield. Common to these is an increased focus on Jesus and on the prayerful seeking of God. These are gifts to be commended to the entire Church.[47]

> ### A story: The Order of Mission (TOM)
> *TOM was inaugurated on 6 April 2003 in a service led by the Archbishop of York. About 30 people took vows. Recognizing that the Church in the West finds itself in a missionary*

context, TOM was created to support people called as leaders in mission to plant missionary churches. It aims not to remove people from the context in which God has called them to serve – often secular employment.

Members embrace a rule of life of simplicity, purity and accountability, as an authentic contemporary expression of ancient vows. The pattern of life is expressed through five common daily times of prayer. Accountability within the Order, and to the wider Church, is structured through the offices of . the Superior, Visitors, Guardians, and Seniors. Individuals may be involved with the Order as Temporaries, Permanents or Associates.

TOM is intended to be a global movement with its own indigenous leadership structure in every part of the world where it operates. The home of the Order is in Sheffield.[48]

The emphases of these groups will differ, as did the emphases of historic orders. What can be noted is that some groups, such as the Northumbria Community and the Order of St Thomas, are intentionally mission focused. In some ways, missionary communities and church planting teams have overlapping characteristics. The dynamics of both groups could be shared with great profit. Church planters would gain from the treasures of disciplined spirituality and community. New Mission Orders might learn from the wisdom gained in planting and in missiology.

youth congregations

It is important to distinguish between youth services (worship events that may be occasional, and may or may not be led by young people[49]) and youth congregations (congregation for youth, by youth). Youth congregations often have a weekly pattern, have recognized leaders, pastoral structures and clear mission intentions. Another model centres on an area youth celebration, probably monthly, linked to youth cells in supporting churches. The growing trend for youth worship and the development of youth congregations both demonstrate the difficulty of integrating young people in to the Church of England as we know it.

Although there are some notable examples of youth congregations, in practice there are, as yet, relatively few full-blown youth congregations identified and reported.[50] There are indications of an increase in youth congregations, and an attempt to gain a detailed national view is only just beginning.

A story: Bracknell, Berkshire

Mark Meardon and three musical friends in their twenties took over a youth service in Bracknell. The service, called Eternity, *was previously planned by adults. He says:*

We decided the old format of the youth service had to be scrapped. The 1994 Alternative Carol Service was the rather embarrassing last straw, with worship songs like 'It came upon a midnight clear' played badly on acoustic guitars, sitting on stools, to the tune of 'All along the Watchtower' by Bob Dylan.

On 13 January 1995, with a budget of £20 and a mission to build a community in which people can experience God's love, we held our first Friday evening service. There was some worship, a bit of a talk and an appeal; 40 to 50 came and there were 7 to 8 professions of faith. These kids were the first fruits. What were we to do with them? We arranged an impromptu follow-up for 15 people at the vicarage. The response encouraged us to continue.

A fortnightly Friday Celebration grew in number to 150. The follow-up group became a regular Wednesday small group [worship, open Bibles, prayer in small groups]. At 30 takers Eternity had to move another way. They split down into 'Cell groups'. In 1998 there was still life, growth, diversity and response. The number of Cell groups had grown to eight. A team of leaders grew with some giving their year out to take on aspects of the work.

Evoke, a drop-in café, started in 1997. Beginning just once a month, it grew to two Fridays. Low key, chill out and relationship-based was the style. Yet this young church needed to remain flexible in approach. Evoke numbers began to drop in 1998. The people sensed the youth culture was moving away from café towards dance. The principle behind Evoke was kept – a place where Eternity can build and form relationships with non-believers. But, despite the creativity that had gone into it and the relatively young life it had known, Evoke was allowed to die and Eclipse was born: dance, live DJs, Playstation, and non-alcoholic bar.

The leaders of Eternity believe there is still a long way to go and they will need to stay flexible for the future. As a fresh expression of church, planted for its deanery and recognized *by that body, it seeks a town-wide ministry to young people. The amazing reality, through the schools work, is that 100 per cent of 11–16 year-olds do make some contact with Eternity and the further dream that partly pulls Eternity into its future is that 15–20 per cent of them will be in active contact with a church.*[51]

facing the gap

Many people consider that the number of young people in church has dropped to such dramatically low levels that Anglicanism in England faces serious ongoing numerical decline. In 1998 Revd Paul Simmonds, a Diocesan Mission Adviser, wrote a paper for Coventry Diocese to examine young people's involvement and engagement with the Church. He concluded:

Not only are we struggling to keep and care for young people from church families, we are making only negligible impact on the vast majority of the young people who are unchurched.[52]

Paul Simmonds and others suggest that the Church is primarily set up to minister to the over-40s, at the expense of young people (the phrase 'young people' here includes people in their 20s and early 30s, as well as those in their teens).

In what ways is the Church of England slanted away from the young?

- A pattern of innovation in liturgical revision and musical variety has not (on the whole) been sustained. A generation of young people find Graham Kendrick old-fashioned and *Common Worship* outmoded.

- The average age of ordination for stipendiary ministry in the Church of England is now around 40 years – much later if non-stipendiary (NSM) and ordained local ministers (OLM) are included.[53] Ordained ministers, including NSMs and OLMs, model a Church for the middle-aged. Although one third of the population is under 25 years, the Church of England has very few ordained people in this age group. The Church needs not only to identify potential younger leaders, but also to release and support existing young people who are leaders among their peers.

- Our commitment to the 'parish' calls us to identify with the totality of those entrusted to us. One third of the population is under 25, but one third of church budgets (or even a tenth of church budgets) is not invested in youth and children's ministry.

Other factors:

- Most youth in churches and their youth groups are the children of Christian parents. Only a small proportion is from a non-church background.
- The huge drop in Sunday school attendance means that the number of those available to 'return to us' has plummeted.
- The Church baptizes fewer than one quarter of all babies born, and fewer than 20 per cent return for Confirmation, with a considerable drop-out rate afterwards. Confirmations themselves have reduced by around 60 per cent through the 1980s and 1990s.[54]

It is not an overstatement to say that, overall, the Church of England is not holding, winning or discipling young people. Although there are some exceptions to this pattern, those exceptions are few in number. Those churches where young people are present in numbers make it clear that younger generations are spiritually open, and that resourcing the existing leadership of the young should be paramount.

the response

Youth A Part (GS 1203) was published in 1996 and endorsed by the General Synod. It has become the cornerstone of a vision to take young people seriously. This focus became an integral part of the Themes of the Archbishops' Council. As a result a Youth Strategy document was commended to Synod in November 2002. This coincided with the creation of schemes to train and deploy youth workers at parish level. It included a process that has seen deliberate consultation with young people, together with proposals for a national Youth Evangelism Fund.

Youth A Part seemed optimistic that young people, treated properly, will come back to existing church.

> If young people are taken seriously, respected and truly valued, the gap between church culture and youth culture will decrease and close quite naturally.[55]

When this was written, the phenomenon of 'youth congregations' had only just begun to appear. The National Youth Strategy document, in section B, on 'young people and worship' takes youth congregations very seriously.

> The time has come to draw lessons from these innovative approaches, to recognize that young people's churches or congregations are not alternative or experimental but fully part of the worshipping community of the Church.[56]

church or congregation – does it matter?

The National Strategy has used language of church or congregation. The distinction is helpful. The word 'congregation' suggests both particularity and partiality. It is possible to envisage parishes where youth congregations and adult congregations exist. Both accept each other in their difference and mutual interdependence, and neither expresses the totality of the Church in that place. The view of this report is that both what young people and what older adults do can be equally considered as expressions of healthy, balanced and sustainable church.

is church for youth necessary?

There is no doubt that youth congregations can meet the needs of a particular (youth) culture. Existing and traditional church seldom realizes its own cultural styles and patterns, and fails to appreciate the large cultural gap that needs to be crossed. Many young people inhabit a different world from that expressed in most churches, and for church to connect gospel and church with them, a fresh expression of church is needed, so that they can find and enjoy authentic Christian community, worship and living.

culture or generation?

The idea of a 'generation gap' has been familiar since the 1960s, and probably since the beginning of time. It is described as a generation gap, but this is an inaccurate description of what is happening, particularly in a time of rapid changes in society.

> Young people are growing up in a different world to that experienced by previous generations. The life experiences of young people in modern industrialised societies have changed significantly over the last two decades.[57]

Today's young people are of a different culture, not simply a different age.

> The primary frontier which needs to be crossed in mission to young people is not so much a generation gap as a profound change in culture.[58]

That being the case, the work of church planting among young people has special significance, because they will grow up to be adults with a different culture. In the past, it has been assumed that young people will grow out of 'this phase' and that when they do they will become 'like us'. But that attitude is no longer sustainable or wise. The style and values in existing church are unlikely to become a pattern where today's young people will feel at home. For some, existing patterns of church will be helpful. But for many (or most), even after they are no longer 'young', the existing ways and styles of doing and being church will not be attractive or meaningful. Hence the contemporary and long-term importance of congregations for and by young people.

So Bishop Graham Cray suggested in an address in 1999:[59]

> It follows that 'youth congregations' are not a bridging strategy. They are not a temporary holding camp where young people can be acclimatised to existing church. It is not a bridge to the real thing. These groupings take responsibility for worship, pastoral care, mission and evangelism. To their members they are the only real thing they know. It is an experience of the Church of Jesus Christ.

why so many expressions?

This chapter has recorded a number of different styles or types of church that have emerged in the last decade. They are ways in which the Church of England has sought to engage with the variety of diverse cultures and networks that are part of contemporary life. They reflect our Anglican instinct to be 'how' and 'where' people are, not simply to wait for them to come to us, and the missionary principle of seeking to inculturate the gospel, rather than imposing a single culture or style on the variety of cultures within our society.

Many of these fresh expressions have been motivated by a desire to connect the gospel and church with fresh cultures and unreached people.

> Only creative church planting will do in a society where those with spiritual questions naturally assume that the church is not the place to find the answers, since Christianity has been tried and found wanting.[60]

Some pioneers and leaders have yearned for a more authentic way of living, being and doing church, and this led to fresh thinking about what church can or should be. In part, the story of these expressions of church includes an element of disillusionment with the existing church and its values. In other expressions of church, motivation stems not from disillusionment, but from discovery.

The variety of fresh expressions is an encouraging sign of the creativity of the Spirit in our age. Fresh expressions should not be embraced simply because they are popular or new,[61] but because they are a sign of the work of God and of the kingdom.

Discernment is needed to identify signs of God's kingdom. The use of a particular methodology, inherited or fresh, does not guarantee mature church or the presence of the kingdom. To conclude this chapter we offer some criteria for discerning authentic missionary churches.

five values for missionary churches

The Anglican Consultative Council, followed by the Lambeth Conference, has identified 'Five Marks of Mission'.[62]

Alongside these indicators, we have identified five values of a missionary church. These are intended to offer a framework that can be applied to an existing local church or to any strategy to develop, grow or plant a church or a fresh expression of church.[63] One additional element is assumed rather than specifically identified. That is the credal foundation of any missionary church, congregation or initiative within the Church of England. This report assumes, but does not take for granted that, to be missionary, a church has to proclaim afresh the faith of the Scriptures and the creeds. This is not a 'value' of the church, but the foundation upon which church is built.

● a missionary church is focused on God the Trinity

Worship lies at the heart of a missionary church, and to love and know God as Father, Son and Spirit is its chief inspiration and primary purpose. It worships and serves a missionary God, and understands itself to share in the divine mission. All of its life and activity is undergirded by prayer.

● a missionary church is incarnational

A missionary church seeks to shape itself in relation to the culture in which it is located or to which it is called. Whenever it is called to be cross-cultural then its long-term members or initial team lay aside their cultural preferences about church to allow the emergence of a form or style of church to be shaped by those they are seeking to reach. If a church is long established, then it evaluates itself in relation to the culture of the community it serves, and strips away whatever is not required by the gospel. An incarnational church seeks to be responsive to the activity of the Spirit in its community.

● a missionary church is transformational

A missionary church exists for the transformation of the community that it serves, through the power of the gospel and the Holy Spirit. It is not self-serving, self-seeking or self-focused. The kingdom of God is its goal, and church is understood as a servant and sign of God's kingdom in its community, whether neighbourhood or network.

• a missionary church makes disciples

A missionary church is active in calling people to faith in Jesus Christ, and it is equally committed to the development of a consistent Christian lifestyle appropriate to, but not withdrawn from, the culture or cultures in which it operates. It engages with culture, but also presents a counter-cultural challenge by its corporate life based on the world view and values of the gospel. It encourages the gifting and vocation of all the people of God, and invests in the development of leaders. It is concerned for the transformation of individuals, as well as the transformation of communities.

• a missionary church is relational

In a missionary church, a community of faith is being formed. It is characterized by welcome and hospitality. Its ethos and style are open to change when new members join. Believers are encouraged to establish interdependent relationships with fellow Christians as they grow into Christ. As a community it is aware that it is incomplete without interdependent relationships with other Christian churches and communities. It does not seek to stand alone.

Much more could be said about a missionary church. These five principles provide a broad standard to help discernment at a time when the shape of the Church of England is increasingly varied and in flux. None of these qualities is automatically guaranteed by particular structures of mission or strategies for church or church planting. Neither do any of these qualities automatically flow from a particular church tradition or 'type'. These five marks are not 'pass' or 'fail' criteria, but may be a helpful way of highlighting or identifying a church's missionary purpose and qualities. As mentioned at the start of this chapter, these principles can be applied to either existing or fresh expressions of church.

These values open up the question of an adequate theology for the Church in mission, and this is explored in the next chapter.

some questions for discussion

> How can the Church better respond to Jesus' call to 'go to all peoples everywhere and make them my disciples'? Matthew 28.19[64] (Bible suggestion: Mark 16.14-20).

➢ Which of the expressions of church identified in this chapter do you think would best serve your local area? Are there still other ways of being church that are appropriate to your situation?

➢ Make a list of the liturgical traditions used in your church. How might the riches of our tradition be better used in the mission of your church?

➢ Look at the 'Five Values of a Missionary Church' that are listed at the end of this chapter.

Which of these values most characterize the church of which you are a part?

Which of these values most challenge the church of which you are a part?

➢ This chapter claims that 'the variety of fresh expressions is an encouraging sign of the creativity of the Spirit in our age'.

How can you learn better to discern the creativity of the Spirit in your own communities? Do you have ways of exploring and acknowledging what the Spirit is doing? How will such discernment affect the way your church plans for mission in the future?

chapter 5
theology for a missionary church

This report has so far outlined the changing context for mission that is now common to most Western Christians. We have put emphasis on the demise of Christendom and on the emergence of a network society with a dominant consumerist ethos.

We have also described the role of church planting within the Church of England's response to this missionary challenge. We have outlined the diversity of 'fresh expressions of church' that have been created. We believe that this diversity is both good and necessary. Time alone will tell which of these models is of lasting value, but we see strengths in many of them.

However, the time has come to ensure that any fresh expressions of church that emerge within the Church of England, or are granted a home within it, are undergirded by an adequate ecclesiology (doctrine of the Church).

The Church of England needs to be true to the gospel and its own history, while engaging adequately with the society in which we now live. The intention here is not primarily to provide a blanket theological underpinning for all new forms of church, but to suggest some theological principles that should influence all decisions about the shape of the Church of England at this time of missionary opportunity.

salvation history

the nature and mission of God in creation and redemption

> Any theology of the church must ultimately be rooted in the being and acts of God: the church is first and foremost the people of God, brought into being by God, bound to God, for the glory of God.[1]

When Christians speak of 'God', it is as shorthand for the Holy Trinity.[2] Two things follow from this. First, God has to be understood relationally and communally: 'Father, Son and Holy Spirit, who mutually indwell one another, exist in one another and for one another, in interdependent giving and receiving.'[3] Second, God is a missionary. We would not know God if the Father had not sent the Son in the power of the Spirit.

In fact the mission of God (*missio dei*) itself expresses God's relational nature.

> The communion of the persons of the Trinity is not to be understood as closed in on itself, but rather open in an outgoing movement of generosity. Creation and redemption are the overflow of God's triune life.[4]

The mission of God as creator, through Christ, in the Spirit, is to bring into being, sustain and perfect the whole creation.

The mission of God as redeemer, through Christ, in the Spirit, is to restore and reconcile the fallen creation (Colossians 1.20).

> God's missionary purposes are cosmic in scope, concerned with the restoration of all things, the establishment of shalom, the renewal of creation and the coming of the Kingdom as well as the redemption of fallen humanity and the building of the Church.[5]

The Church is both the fruit of God's mission – those whom he has redeemed, and the agent of his mission – the community through whom he acts for the world's redemption. 'The mission of the Church is the gift of participating through the Holy Spirit in the Son's mission from the Father to the world.'[6]

It is therefore of the essence (the DNA) of the Church to be a missionary community. 'There is Church because there is mission, not vice versa.'[7] Apart from worship, everything else is secondary to this. This sets the standard by which the Church tests all its activity.

It is not the Church of God that has a mission in the world, but the God of mission who has a Church in the world.[8]

Church planting should not, therefore, be church centred. It should not be another device to perpetuate an institution for that institution's own sake. It is to be an expression of the mission of God. 'What is mission if not the engagement with God in the entire enterprise of bringing the whole of creation to its intended destiny? A local church cannot claim to be part of this if it only serves itself.'[9]

Mission comes from the Father, through the Son in the power of the Spirit. The Son himself, through incarnation, atonement, resurrection and ascension, is the sole foundation of the Church.[10] We are stewards of a gospel that tells what he has done.

The Son of God expressed this mission in terms of the kingdom of God. The kingdom is a divine activity whereas the Church is a human community. Kingdom agenda and values are often more radical than church readily allows. In bringing the kingdom, God is on the move and the Church is always catching up with him. We join his mission. We should not invite him to join ours.

It is the work of the Spirit to empower the Church to preach and embody that gospel in ways appropriate to each cultural context.

> In a world of ever increasing social complexity the church cannot simply adhere to fixed traditional forms. It must reach more and more deeply into its own realities and dynamics within the purposes of God for the world, and invite the Holy Spirit to stir its heart, soul, mind and strength. If it does so, it will learn to participate more fully in the energy of the Spirit of Christ by which God, through his church, is drawing all human society to its fulfilment in the kingdom of God.[11]

The mutual ministries of the Son of God and the Spirit of God are essential to a Christian understanding of the relationship between gospel and culture. Although the Son of God became a human being within one particular culture, the eternal salvation he won is universally offered to all cultures. The Spirit, through whom the Son became incarnate[12] and through whom he offered himself for our salvation,[13] inspires and directs the particular form the gospel community takes within each culture.

christ and culture

The diversity of creation, through Christ, with its diversity of human cultures and communities, gives a further indication of the appropriateness of diversity in expressions of church.

For example, the second-century Christian apologist, Justin Martyr, spoke of people's ability to grasp parts of the truth even before Christ's coming because they possessed 'seeds of the Word'. At Christ's coming the *Logos spermatikos* or 'seed-bearing Word' took shape and was made human.[14] Justin reconciled elements of Greek thought with Christianity by asserting that, while the Church had the complete truth, there were also truths of philosophy that might be attributed to the working of the same *Logos* who revealed all truth in his incarnate life and was both the creative Word and (as the Stoics taught) the divine Reason.

This dialogue between the eternal Word and particular human cultures has been going on implicitly since the creation of the world. It is this same process that is continued and intensified with the proclamation of the Word become flesh.[15] Hence conversion ought not to involve the transfer of individuals from their native culture to the culture of the Church, so much as the conversion of their culture enriching the cultural life of the Church.

the work of Christ – incarnation, cross and resurrection

incarnation – a world to enter

The incarnation of God in Christ is unique. Only God can take human nature for our salvation. God in Christ entered the world, taking on a specific cultural identity. The revelation of God for all cultures was embodied in one particular culture. If cultural solidarity with the Palestinian communities of his day was a necessary aspect of Christ's mission, the same principle applies to us.[16] Moreover, the early Christians did not remain culturally static, but quickly translated the gospel out of the original language and culture of Jesus, as the Church was planted into non-Jewish cultures.[17] The gospel can only be proclaimed in a culture, not at a culture.

> If the church is to be in a position to offer all men the mystery of salvation and the life brought by God, then it must implant itself among all these groups in the same way that Christ by his incarnation committed himself to the particular social and cultural circumstances of the men among whom he lived.[18]

the cross – a world to counter

But, 'the incarnation of divine love in a world of sin leads to the cross'.[19] Jesus belonged to his own culture and yet was prophetically critical of it. His life of faithful obedience to his Father, in his culture, led to his death. It is through his death and resurrection that he was shown to be the universal Lord who is able to belong to and challenge the cultures of every time and place.[20] The incarnation should never be separated from the cross. In the same way, Christians are called to live, within each culture, under the lordship of Christ, irrespective of the cost.

A truly incarnational Church is one that imitates, through the Spirit, both Christ's loving identification with his culture and his costly counter-cultural stance within it. His announcement of, and promise of, God's kingdom cannot be separated from his call to repentance, as the price of entry. Following his example, his Church is called to loving identification with those to whom it is sent, and to exemplify the way of life to which those who repent turn. Otherwise its call to repentance is reduced to detached moralizing.

incarnation and cross – a missionary exchange

St Paul describes Christ's work in terms of an 'exchange'.[21] This was summarized by Irenaeus as 'Christ became what we are in order that we might become what he is'.[22] Paul uses this same pattern for his own work of mission. He becomes what those he seeks to evangelize are, so that they can share in the salvation he has found. Here, incarnation and cross combine to provide a model for the practice of mission and the planting of the Church.[23]

> The incarnation involves an exchange, the dignity and power of which it is humanly impossible to grasp, only faith can give us a tiny glimpse of its reality: God becomes one of us, even to the extent that he accepts suffering and death . . . This exchange is relived every time there is an act of inculturation. God in Christ enters more fully into our human condition; we share more fully in his life. We die in Christ to that which is sinful and we rise to a creative newness in human relationships through the transforming power of Christ.[24]

The concept of 'incarnation' has tended to be used by Western Anglicans to emphasize only one part of the dynamic of the Son's Incarnation. Usage is mainly concerned with a vulnerable identification with others, being accessible to them and accepting them. There is far less emphasis placed on the radical cost to the Son.

This process of God's self-sacrifice was a subject of early Christian worship, celebrated in Philippians 2. Here, the eternal Son, who willingly takes the form of a dying crucified servant, is both a subject of praise and is commended as a pattern for relationships. While St Paul is primarily speaking of relationships within the Church, the principle must extend to that between the Church and the world beyond, for that is precisely the relationship for which the Son took flesh. St John tells of the risen Jesus commissioning his apostles, 'As the Father has sent me, so I send you.'[25]

This is also made explicit in 1 Corinthians 9.19ff. Here Paul uses the same *doulos* word used in Philippians 2 to refer to his own practice as a missionary. There is a real parallel in both the style of the passage and the patterning of his own behaviour as a missionary after that of Christ.[26] Paul gives up his freedom as Christ gave up his glory, in order to win people. The practical result is the entering of another culture.

The Son's self-emptying, from one perspective, involves a great and costly change. But St Paul, in Philippians, also insists that it is the revelation of the true nature of the living God. If it is the nature of God's love to undertake such sacrifice, it must also be the nature of his Church. The Church is most true to itself when it gives itself up, in current cultural form, to be re-formed among those who do not know God's Son. In each new context the Church must die to live.

resurrection – a world to anticipate

In the New Testament the resurrection is both a unique act of God in history, providing the basis for Christian hope,[27] and a power released into the world.[28] Because Christ has been raised we will be raised. But we live now in the power of the resurrection. Because of the resurrection our work for Christ is not in vain but is potentially of eternal value.[29] The key expression is 'first fruits'. This is used both of the resurrection and of the gift of the Spirit.[30] The first part of the harvest of the last day, the promised new heaven and earth, is in the world now. Churches can be pointers to God's promised future. They are to be sources of hope, imperfect local pilot plants of God's future world.

the Spirit of Christ

The Scriptures, particularly the New Testament centred on Christ, may be regarded as a gift of God from the past. They are to be guarded and passed on, as the only foundation for the Church.[31] But when we discern the work of the Spirit in our churches today, we may recognize this creative and reconciling work as the missionary God's gift to us from the future that is already prepared for us. For the Spirit makes known to us the foretaste and first fruits of the coming kingdom.[32] The Spirit brings into being, in and through the Church, anticipations of things that Scripture promises for the Last Day.[33]

When the Spirit descended at Pentecost, people of many nations heard the gospel proclaimed in their own languages. The Spirit brings to light at the birth of the Church the way by which the Church is to grow – not by imposing conformity but by 'translating the message' into each language – including the languages of culture.[34]

God's kingdom is where the blind see, the deaf hear and the lame dance for joy. It is a future in which justice comes for the poor, peace to the nations and all visions of race, culture and national identity disappear as we discover we are all family together and we worship our God for ever.[35] As the Spirit provides the first fruits of the coming kingdom, the Spirit makes it possible to experience something of this kingdom unity within the present diverse body of the Church.[36]

The Church takes its missionary form through receiving the gifts of the past and the future. At a time of substantial change, the Church of England needs to learn from the Spirit to be more an anticipation of God's future than a society for the preservation of the past. Perhaps our greatest need is of a baptism of imagination about the forms of the Church.

> The Spirit enables fidelity to and continuity with apostolic faith but constantly actualises and particularises this tradition afresh in the present, so that the truth of Christ is brought alive for ever in new situations with which the church engages in its missionary calling. This is integral to the Spirit's eschatological ministry – to carry the church forward in mission, anticipating here and now in ever-fresh ways the Father's final eschatological desire.[37]

Christ and culture – inculturation/contextualization

Despite the substantial work done on 'Gospel and Culture' in recent years, the Church of England has not yet drawn significantly upon the world Church's experience in cross-cultural mission. 'Inculturation' (the Roman Catholic term) and 'contextualization' (preferred by many evangelicals) have been treated as of limited relevance, appropriate only to those preparing to serve overseas. This is due, in part, to assumptions about Christendom, blinding our imaginations about the form of the Church.

In 1997 a Lausanne Consultation spoke of moving 'from contextualization as a strategy for cross-cultural mission to contextualization as a necessary practice of all churches in mission within their own cultures'.[38] This recognizes that no society is culture-neutral. Every culture, including our own, needs the transforming challenge of the gospel. This is all the more vital since different networks within our post-Christendom, consumer society, are often culturally worlds away from each other. Our society is changing so fast that it is becoming a new missionary context in which many members of the Church of England experience mission in their own land as cross-cultural.

Any theology concerning the nature and shape of the Church in a new missionary context must address the appropriate place of culture in shaping the Church.

A faithful Church is continually shaped by its inner dynamic: the flow of Apostolic Tradition, with Scripture as its norm. The Church is, however, also shaped by the kind of world in which it finds itself. This must mean a constant receiving of the Gospel into our particular context.[39]

There is a three-way conversation to be had in every serious attempt at inculturation.[40] The conversation partners are: the historic gospel, uniquely revealed in Holy Scripture and embodied in the Catholic creeds; the Church, which is engaging in mission, with its own particular culture and history; the culture within which the gospel is being shared.[41]

All three are needed to form a church embodying the gospel in a way appropriate to the local context.

It is not possible for a missionary/evangeliser to 'do inculturation' by analysing the culture to be evangelised and reinterpreting the Christian message in its light. Such a process could only result in a superficial adaptation of the gospel 'from above'. Inculturation is essentially a community process 'from below'.[42]

Its purpose is to allow the gospel to transform a culture from within. No serious attempt at inculturation by the Church of England can begin with a fixed view of the outward form of the local church. In practice, 'there are many who still fuse the meaning and the forms of the gospel'.[43]

The Spirit does not simply bring life to an already predetermined structure, but constantly transforms the community in the present, relating it to Christ, its members to each other and its members to the world in ways which are appropriate to the ever changing circumstances in which the church finds itself.[44]

the challenge of syncretism

All attempts at inculturation struggle with the danger of syncretism.[45] 'In the attempt to be "relevant" one may fall into syncretism, and in the effort to avoid syncretism one may become irrelevant.'[46] Britain at the start of the third millennium is predominantly a consumer society. The missionary challenge is to embody the Church within it, while also challenging the prevailing consumerist pattern. Inculturation seeks the gospel transformation of a society from within, and so a distinctive Christian lifestyle in a consumer society is fundamental to the task. 'The everyday challenge of consumerism is yet to be fully acknowledged by most Christian communities.'[47]

The willingness to 'die to live' provides one key to this challenge. A commitment to lay aside one's own preferences, give priority to a different culture, and work with those in it to discover how to express an authentic shared life in Christ, is the opposite of self-centred consumerism. To live under the lordship of Christ is to exercise our powers of choice in submission to his will, as we seek the interests of others.[48]

This process is required of all new planting initiatives, whether the cultural differences are large or small. This is clearly seen in St Paul's strategy described in 1 Corinthians 9. Although at home with his Jewish culture, his approach is 'to the Jew I became *as* a Jew'. His identity is now found in the Messiah. This puts a critical distance between him and his former way of life, and, at the same time, frees him to enter and value other cultures. When ministering to 'those outside the law' he becomes 'as one outside the law' (but 'under Christ's law'). All this is done 'for the sake of the gospel',[49] which he has received, and is bound to pass on, unchanged.[50]

A story

Vincent Donovan was an American Catholic missionary to the Masai – the noble nomadic people of East Africa – in the 1960s. No one had had success in evangelization among them. They would not come and stay at the mission compound. Education and health facilities did not draw them. Donovan resolved he would have to go to them, on their terms. His book Christianity Rediscovered *tells of his struggles as he discovered how to be both faithful to Orthodoxy and Scripture, and to recast the vocabulary of the gospel story to communicate with the Masai in their culture.*

But even when groups, usually by common debated consent, chose to follow Christ, still church among them had to be formed. From what they knew of gospel values, they had to be allowed to form church in their culture – even deciding what word or phrase they would use for 'church'. It was a case of their making it up, as they went along, and the Holy Spirit being trusted to do that work among them, with Donovan acting as a consultant but not director.

Significant cultural challenges arose. A notable example was that Masai men and women do not eat meals together. Communion then raised very basic issues. But the converted Masai understood that the change of their beliefs included that Christ made different kinds of people one, because they

were equally loved, and this pattern would have to change.
So men and women of the Masai 'brotherhood of God' (their
name for church) ate together for the first time – ever. It could
only have happened if they decided it should be so. The life
and discipline of the emerging church took shape by the
creative apostolic task of double listening to the gospel and
the culture.

Vincent Donovan saw the process of inculturation as having the potential to create a pointer to God's future. His apostolic comment on encountering youth of the West was:

do not try to call them back to where they were, and do not try to call them to where you are, beautiful as that place may seem to you. You must have the courage to go with them to a place that neither you nor they have been before.[51]

the Church is designed to reproduce

The theology of inculturation makes use of the biblical botanical metaphors of sowing and reaping, emphasizing in particular the need of a seed to fall into the ground and die, or it remains alone. The underlying assumption is that the Church is God's community with a divine mandate to reproduce. It is intended by God to multiply, by the Spirit, and to fill all creation.[52] This is an essential dimension of any missionary ecclesiology. Churches are created by God to grow.

We do not argue that it is the natural condition for every local church to be growing. But we do argue that it is the normative condition for the national church in normal times if it keeps the faith and keeps up with the culture.[53]

the genesis of the Church

The human race was created to be a community in unbroken relationship with God, with a mandate to govern the earth with justice. From its inception, God's human community was to reproduce itself biologically, in order to fulfil the divine purpose (Genesis 1.28). Jesus, the Lord of the Church, is called the 'Second Adam' in the New Testament. The Church is intended to be a new humanity, which is to reproduce itself through mission, and so fill the earth.

the covenant challenge to the Church

The covenant with Abraham focused God's purpose for humanity in the future of one family. They were to multiply to be as numerous 'as the stars of heaven and as the sand that is on the seashore'.[54] But this community did not exist for itself. Through them 'all the families of the earth' would be blessed.[55] John 8 and Galatians 3 see Jesus' followers as the true children of Abraham, in fulfilment of the Genesis promises.

> The church is the pilgrim people of God. It is on the move, hastening to the ends of the earth to beseech all men to be reconciled to God, and hastening to the end of time to meet its Lord who will gather all into one. Therefore the nature of the church is never to be defined in static terms, but only in terms of that to which it is going. It cannot be understood rightly except in a perspective which is at once missionary and eschatological.[56]

From the Patriarchs until the conquest of the Promised Land, the Old Testament people of God are seen as a pilgrim people, a people continually on the move, with a tent as the focus of the divine presence. Once settled in the land, their understanding of God's presence becomes focused on a fixed location, the Temple. After the destruction of the first Temple, there follows a time of exile. Life in post-Christendom has many dimensions of exile.[57] While Christ is the fulfilment of both tent and temple, perhaps the tent imagery is more appropriate for our time.

Jesus, the Church and the kingdom

The church is a sign and disclosure of the kingdom of God. The kingdom has certain clear qualities – its breaking of social boundaries, its hope for the poor, its message of God's welcome for all, focused in Christ. But it is also presented as something that grows. In particular, a good number of the parables of the kingdom concern reproductive growth. In John 15 Jesus and his disciples fulfil the Old Testament picture of the people of God as a Vine. The purpose of remaining in Christ is to bear fruit to the Father's glory. A tree bears fruit to reproduce itself. So it is with Christ and the Church.

the story of the young Church – Acts and Epistles

The story of Acts is not simply a general one of mission, but a more specific one of church reproduction or the planting process. After Antioch (Acts 13) 'church planting' becomes an evident pattern – the starting of new communities, containing both Jews and Gentiles. That came through the

Spirit's vision given to Peter (Acts 10) and the missionary call of Paul (Acts 9). But the vision for reproduction was written into both the Great Commission in Matthew 28[58] and the Lukan purpose of the Spirit (Acts 1.8).[59] Both presuppose that the Church is to be reproduced, by disciples from and in as many ethnic groups as there are in the world.[60]

In Romans 15.23 Paul explains why he is moving on. He says there is 'no further place for me in these regions' and (vv. 18f) 'by word and deed, by the power of signs and wonders, by the power of the Spirit of God . . . I have fully proclaimed the good news of Christ'.

> What, exactly, has Paul done? Certainly not converted all the populations of those regions. Certainly not solved their social and economic problems. He has in his own words 'fully preached the gospel' and left behind communities of men and women who believe the gospel and live by it.[61]

Church planting is at the heart of the Pauline mission.

Ephesians 4 lists Christ-given ministries: apostles, prophets, evangelists, pastors/teachers. Although the term has wider meaning, apostles plant churches. Planting establishes the community from which further apostolic, prophetic and evangelistic ministry proceeds and which, through pastoring and teaching, grows to maturity in Christ.

The story of the young Church, and the dynamics by which it came to birth, bear witness to a Church born to reproduce; not just planting churches but with an ecclesiological instinct for furthering God's mission.

the ultimate destiny of the Church

To see the Church as the 'reproducing community' helps it to realize that its task, in each generation, is necessarily incomplete. Only in heaven will mission and planting cease. Growth, by reproduction, will be vital to fill the earth.

The Church is also called to be a foretaste of the coming kingdom. It is more an imperfect anticipation of God's future world than a preservation of earlier cultural forms.

> The church does more than merely point to a reality beyond itself. By virtue of its participation in the life of God, it is not only a sign and instrument, but also a genuine foretaste of God's Kingdom, called to show forth visibly, in the midst of history, God's final purposes for humankind.[62]

As such it is always incomplete. The inevitable weakness and sinfulness of the Church at any particular time cannot simply be excused, but it is, through God's grace, the place where forgiveness and the power for a change of life can be seen and experienced.

the marks of the Church

The four classic marks of the Church, enshrined in the Nicene Creed as 'one, holy, catholic, and apostolic', remind the Church of its true nature and calling. They can act as a call to repentance because they all also reflect the Church's missionary vocation.

the Church is ONE

The Church is one through baptism, which is an integral dimension of mission. Mission creates unity within a diversity of cultures. 'Go therefore and make disciples of all nations, baptizing them in the name of the Father and of the Son and of the Holy Spirit.'[63]

Reproduction is not cloning. It does not mean 'more of the same'. It involves the imaginative ability to take on a diversity of appropriate forms in different cultures. Once again the Trinity provides the living example of unity in diversity.

The diversity within unity of the one God also provides a model for the relationships between churches. Fresh expressions of church and more traditional forms should live in interdependence. This has a particular importance in a multi-layered network society.

The term *perichoresis* conveys the interrelationship and interconnectedness of the persons of the Trinity.

> The three persons of the Trinity in perichoretic relationship do not simply take up an attitude of loving concern towards each other, but actually make each other who they are through living relation.[64]

No Christian group can legitimately think 'we exist by ourselves, or for ourselves'. This applies equally to emerging and inherited forms of church. Here the understanding of oneness is closely linked to that of catholicity.

the Church is HOLY

The Church is holy because it is set apart for God and for God's missionary purposes in history. 'You are a chosen race, a royal priesthood, a holy nation, God's own people, in order that you may proclaim the mighty acts of him who called you out of darkness into his marvellous light.'[65] A Church that is separate, even distinctive, but not involved in the mission of its Lord, cannot claim to be holy.

Holiness as separation for God's purposes leads to the call to a distinctively holy life. At the heart of such holiness is the willingness to die to one's own comfort and preferences and be made alive to God's. It is a holy Church that is willing to die to its own culture in order to live for God in another.

the Church is CATHOLIC

The word catholic means that which accords to wholeness.[66]

Rather than implying a global or national uniformity, catholicity is an invitation to inclusion. Catholicity is only complete when the Church is made up from 'every tribe and language and people and nation'.[67]

Catholicity refers to the universal scope of the church as a society instituted by God in which all sorts and conditions of humanity, all races, nations and cultures, can find a welcome and a home. Catholicity therefore suggests that the church has the capacity to embrace diverse ways of believing and worshipping, and that this diversity comes about through the 'incarnation' of Christian truth in many different cultural forms which it both critiques and affirms. The catholicity of the church is actually a mandate for cultural hospitality.[68]

Catholicity provides a challenge to the local church or churches for diversity within mission. It is an invitation to church planting and fresh expressions of church.

The agenda of the local church must always be to include rather than exclude. Unconsciously churches reject large tracts of humanity by failing to make provision for them to find a 'space' which they can occupy without automatically denying their culture, music, way of speech, or capacity to handle texts and concepts.[69]

But catholicity also implies that there are limits to diversity. The gospel may have many clothes, but there is only one gospel. Christ was and is for all people, at all times and in all places. But it is only Christ as revealed in the Scriptures who has power to save.

When catholicity is understood as an invitation to cultural hospitality, effective Christian mission will inevitably raise questions of unity and of reconciliation. In the New Testament it was the Gentile mission (preaching the gospel to people 'not like us') that led both to a necessary diversity in the New Testament Church, and to conflict and a challenge to reconciliation.

True Christian unity and reconciliation result in an enriched Church. This can only happen if time is first allowed for a new plant or expression of church to establish its own identity. Then both churches can enrich one another as 'adults'. The alternative would be absorption.

Dying to live has then two dimensions: first the missionaries' willingness to die to their own preferred forms; then the determination of the 'parent' church not to impose its own culture on the emerging church, but to allow it to mature, and then be open to mutual enrichment.

the Church is APOSTOLIC

Apostolicity is the true source of the Church's unity and catholicity. It is the safeguard that prevents inculturation becoming syncretism.

> Apostolicity is the link between the definitive original message and mission of the Apostles whom Jesus Christ first commissioned and the tasks of the church today. It refers to the dynamic continuity and spiritual faithfulness of the church in mission.[70]

At the same time, it is the mark that continually presses the Church to engage culture with the gospel. The Church is sent into the world with a message to live and share. 'Apostolicity requires obedience to the original and fundamental apostolic witness by reinterpretation to meet the needs of each new situation.'[71]

The Church must model the apostolic nature of Christ, if it is to be genuinely Christian. Being apostolic is equally about a future direction as it is about an authorized past. What might it mean then to call the Church apostolic? It is apostolic in that it was sent by Jesus: 'so I send you'. But there is more than this functional connection. The Church is apostolic because Jesus was apostolic first. 'As the Father has sent me . . .'.[72] 'In Christ, God was his own apostle.'[73]

a model for health?

Study of the four marks of the Church must not be so complex that local church leaders dismiss their importance. We need ways to work with the essence of the marks that help us with the task of healthy growth as well as validation. It may help to present the four marks as being like four dimensions of a journey, none of which exists without reference to the others.

All expressions of church are drawn into a journey with an **UP** dimension – the journey toward God in worship, which must equally be about seeking God and about becoming like God in holiness. Without the transformation that should gradually result, we are only playing liturgical games or having charismatic caresses. Then our worship and witness will be hollow. The **UP** dimension provides an expression of the Church seeking to be Holy.

The Church is led into a journey containing an **IN** dimension. It is a dimension of relationships, in order to express, in practice, the oneness of the Trinity and of the body of Christ. The persons of the Trinity show us the quality of diversity held in unity because of their eternal love. Unless such love is the base of oneness in community, gatherings of the church, at whatever size, and of whatever antiquity, will only be held together by organizational artificial glue. The **IN** dimension demonstrates the Church seeking to express Oneness.

The nature of the Church includes being sent onto the journey **OUT**. The sending in mission embraces with the breadth of the five marks of mission.[74] This journey on and out is fulfilment of our apostolic call; we but follow Jesus the Apostle. Without this the Church is not only in danger of introspection, becoming fixed and complacent, but enters the realm of disobedience, ignoring the call of the missionary God. The **OUT** dimension manifests the Church seeking to be Apostolic.

To be church, we are called to walk a journey that has an **OF** dimension. No one exists for themselves, or by themselves. All came from some part of the wider Church. They are called to relate together. This connects local church to the wider Church now. **OF** also celebrates the connection of the Church militant to the Church triumphant. We have a history of which to be proud, in part, and from which to learn. Both the Church militant and triumphant are expressions of interdependence in the **OF** dimension as the Church seeks signs of being Catholic.

Anglican ecclesiology and 'fresh expressions' of church

None of the above is alien to Anglicanism. The Church of England identifies itself as 'part of the One, Holy, Catholic and Apostolic Church'. It claims to be a participant in the mainstream of historic Christianity and shares the

Catholic creeds with all Trinitarian Churches. Many of the authors quoted above are Anglican. Nevertheless, Anglicanism also has a distinctive testimony and tradition within the Christian Church.

Engagement in the dynamics of its theological and practical formation is one of the distinctive features of the Church in Anglicanism: there is no straightforward 'doctrine of the Church' but an ongoing theological formation of church life.[75]

the Declaration of Assent

Leaders of any Anglican expression of church should be able to make the Declaration of Assent[76] in good conscience. Commitment to the historic Christian faith, as the Church of England has received it, is more important than adherence to any particular cultural expression of Anglican faith. Indeed, the charge is to confess the 'faith the Church is called upon to proclaim afresh in each generation'.

During a time of cultural stability this commitment is primarily a matter of stewardship of the faith and practice of the past. But, in a time of major cultural change, as this report suggests, 'to proclaim afresh' implies change – possibly radical change – in the shape of the Church.

> To proclaim afresh cannot simply mean saying the same words to a new generation that were said to previous generations, in order to draw them into churches which were shaped by modernity and the closing decades of Christendom.[77]

the Lambeth Quadrilateral

As part of a worldwide Church, Anglicanism prefers to seek unity within tolerated diversity. The practice of the Anglican Communion is helpful and contextual cultural divergence in different provinces is welcome. Yet, at the same time, an instinct for loose common features, a common consultative council, all held not least by relational bonds between bishops, may be one that will need increased application within, not just beyond, the Church of England. The Chicago-Lambeth 1888 Quadrilateral of Scripture, the Creeds, the dominical sacraments and the Historic Episcopacy provide a similar yardstick for a common understanding of church. We have already discussed Scripture and creed, but sacraments and episcopacy are also important.

the dominical sacraments

The sacraments of baptism and Eucharist are 'pledges of the New Covenant'. 'A sacrament is about establishing commitment and relationship.'[78] A mission initiative that does not have an authorized practice of baptism and the celebration of the Eucharist is not yet a 'church' as Anglicans understand it.

Churches are eucharistic communities, irrespective of their church tradition, or the frequency of eucharistic worship. The Eucharist lies at the heart of Christian life. It is the act of worship (including the ministry of the Word) in which the central core of the biblical gospel is retold and re-enacted. New expressions of church may raise practical difficulties about authorized ministry, but, if they are to endure, they must celebrate the Eucharist.

episcopacy

The role of the 'bishop in mission' was explored in some depth at the 1998 Lambeth Conference, and is here considered in detail in Chapter 7 – 'An enabling framework for a missionary church'.[79]

The bishop's role as missionary, focus of unity and guardian of the faith, places him necessarily in a key strategic role. It is said that the Church of England is 'episcopally led and synodically governed'. In council and in synod the bishop leads the Church in its decision making and he licenses ministers. This is a missionary role, necessarily responsive to cultural change. 'The historic episcopate is locally adapted in the methods of its administration to the varying needs of the nations and peoples called of God into the unity of his Church.'[80]

This means that proper relationship with the bishop of the diocese becomes crucial. To be 'in communion' with the diocesan bishop and hold his licence becomes a theological as well as practical necessity. To be Anglican is to be in communion with the See of Canterbury, and, at a diocesan level, with one's own bishop. *Breaking New Ground* identified this as an important principle:

> The episcopate represents the church's catholicity.[81]

a national Church

We have already shown how a network society changes the nature of many local communities and thus of the parochial system. The parochial system was established to embody a gospel priority. At the heart of that system is a commitment to 'the cure of souls'. The Church of England establishes parishes, plants churches and licenses ministers because of its commitment to the eternal salvation and pastoral well-being of the whole nation. Ministers share the bishop's cure of souls. As the shape of community changes it is the bishop's responsibility to license ministry to new areas and new patterns of community. Otherwise our commitment to the nation will not be met, and the incarnational principle undermined.

a shared family

An Anglican is someone who is part of the Anglican body of the Christian family. They share in the same history, whether baptized into it, or adopted later in the Christian journey. As part of the family there are valued relationships. These are at every level from the local small group, in the local church, the parish, with the deanery, the diocese, the province and the Communion. The relationships involve authority and responsibility.

If there is concern within the local church, appeal can be made to the wider family. The local church also has a responsibility to the wider family to go along with shared agreements (in Synods, Canons and so on) and to play its part financially. While these relationships can in part be stated in legal terms, they go far beyond the legal.

a time to reflect on experience

> Mission is the mother of theology . . . Theology began as an accompanying manifestation of the Christian mission.[82]

Christian theology reflects upon experience in the light of God's revelation in Christ. At any significant time of cultural change, both the new context and the resulting Christian mission raise new questions. Some old methodologies fail, many familiar patterns change. But new discoveries are made and new patterns of ministry and mission begin to emerge. There is continuity and discontinuity.

The working group believes that we are at such a time in the mission of the Church of England.

some questions for discussion

➤ Why do you think a God of mission has given us the Church? (Bible suggestion: Acts 2.43-47.)

➤ Where can you see the God of mission already at work in your own context, and in what ways does your local church need to catch up with what God is doing?

List the ways in which your church can be identified as one, holy, catholic and apostolic. Are some of these attributes of the Church more prominent than others? What more could you do to show people outside the Church that these marks are what God calls the Church to be?

➤ This chapter says that 'Jesus belonged to his own culture, yet was prophetically critical of it'. What do you think the role of prophetic criticism has in today's Church and how can it become part of your mission strategy? What role can a prophetic ministry have in your own fresh expressions of church?

➤ This chapter quotes Tim Dearborn, 'It is not the Church of God that has a mission in the world, but the God of mission who has a Church in the world.'[83] In what ways do we practise obedience to God's will and are our mission strategies ever in danger of getting God to validate what *we* think is right? In what ways do we make sure we are listening to God?

some methodologies for a missionary church

This chapter offers some principles for any church seeking to develop a fresh approach to doing and being church, either as a new initiative, or else as a new orientation for the sake of mission. Setting down what has worked in practice, and relating this to our ideas about mission and the Church, can help in planning and assessing styles and types of church.

There is a flood of books on 'new ways of being church'. How 'church' is understood, and what 'church' is, are subject to close scrutiny. Within that framework there is considerable interest in how the Church can be more missionary, and how to encourage churches that reflect the context and culture in which they develop.

other sources

This report can only outline some key aspects of good practice and mission methodology. Practitioners and permission-givers are strongly advised to read the recommended books.[1] By contrast to ten years ago, there are now tested higher education modules on church planting, some at postgraduate level, of which some are offered in block weeks to make them accessible to people in programmes of in-service training.[2]

Other useful sources are available, but not in book form. These texts are available on www.encountersontheedge.org.uk. They include a church planting good practice guide (written for the Church Army's evangelists who have this focus to their work), lessons from weak and failed plants and how to help them (based on the consultancy experience of Anglican Church Planting Initiatives),[3] and practical steps and insights for those planning a plant, and for the early life of a plant (also from Anglican Church Planting Initiatives).

general methodology

double listening

This process involves listening to the culture where a church might be established, and to the inherited tradition of the gospel and the church.

It is the starting point for determining what form a new church might take.

For church planting, listening to both contemporary culture and to church tradition is vital. The planters – here understood in the simple generic sense of those involved in the starting and sustaining of further and fresh communities of faith – carry with them an existing understanding of the faith and of church. They do not come with empty hands, but the next task is to have open ears. Attention to the mission context, or listening to the world, comes before discerning how the inherited Christian tradition works within it. Mission precedes the shape of the church that will be the result, when the seed of the gospel roots in the mission culture. Listening to the context of the world shapes what emerges. Then the second aspect of double listening validates it, through connection with the faith uniquely revealed in the Scriptures.

Double listening is a process that enables something to evolve as its context changes. It seeks to hold in tension both a creative engagement with context and a faithfulness to the good news in Jesus.

> A good case can be made for [evolution] being the best single word summary of an Anglican approach to change. It suggests creativity, responsiveness to present environment, and the ability to work at a theme [or tradition].[4]

An example of this approach is Bishop Michael Nazir-Ali's book *Shapes of the Church to Come* – especially chapters 1 and 2, which demonstrate an extended form of double listening.[5]

context should shape the church

This approach, explicitly followed in best church planting practice, is a pattern for the whole Church. In the past, two tendencies have caused problems. Firstly, like nineteenth-century missionaries, some planters have uncritically imported their preferred existing model of being church, and imposed this on situations where that model was not appropriate.

Secondly, many of the models of church planting described in this chapter were popularized from the late 1980s, but little priority was attached to them. It has taken the planting movement time to realize this has been unhelpful.

Viewed in the light of wider experience, it is as though church planting has three dimensions. Different models or categories of church planting can be arranged to illustrate those dimensions, but each dimension is vital. Similarly, the order in which each dimension is considered is important.

The first dimension has little to do with the shape of the church, and everything to do with the process of engaging in mission, which will eventually help determine choices about church.

the first dimension: who is the plant *for*?

Any proposal to begin a church plant or fresh expression of church should start by identifying its mission goals. In keeping with the analogy of three dimensions, this can be described as the **width** of what is being chosen, created and shaped.

is it for neighbourhood or network?

Breaking New Ground has laid the foundations for the necessity and validity of working with aspects both of English life and culture.

> It is possible to see that networks are now the communities to which people feel a predominant loyalty.[6]

> We need . . . to find ways to enable diverse styles of church life to co-exist without always having recourse to territorial or even denominational boundaries. Here the church planting movement has much to teach us. Further, an episcopal church is well placed to discern when (in order to be rooted in the community) the focus on parochial territory needs supplementing with a realistic awareness of network and neighbourhood.[7]

This issue matters because different evangelism and planting strategies and contacts are needed to work with neighbourhoods or with networks. They function in different ways and at different paces. Team leaders will need different team sizes and mixes of gifts. For example, experience has shown that to do network church well needs larger teams than is required by some neighbourhood-oriented expressions of church. Church for network may demand a higher level of creativity and presentation because the younger generations typically found in network society are looking for quality, not just informality, in public meetings. Similarly, different permissions from church authorities are required. The two resultant churches may need different legal entities. They represent equally important but significantly different mission tasks, with differing church outcomes.

is it for the non-churched or the de-churched?

The de-churched have some first-hand experience of church in their lifetime, though they have now left. The non-churched have never been and don't want to go. Sensitive survey work can help to grow an understanding of the proportions of these two groups that might be encountered. Anecdotal evidence will also exist in a prospective planting team through their knowledge of their networked group of friends.

Most current evangelistic strategies have most impact among the de-churched. Most church members only know how to do evangelism with the de-churched. Working with the non-churched means starting much 'further back', and expecting to have to work for far longer in building aspects of community before seeing results in terms of any spiritual interest. Stories that illustrate both the difficulties and encouragements of developing church among the non-churched can be found in the series from the Church Army's Sheffield Centre, 'Encounters on the Edge'.[8]

is it for a specific cultural group?
'Culture' does not just apply to ethnic groups. It is relevant to the creation of (for example) generation-specific churches, or church for deaf people. It could be a dimension of work among the homeless, or church for the shut-in elderly. Some towns and cities are ethnically very diverse, but across the country there are many varieties of non-ethnic culture, class and lifestyle. The phrase 'unreached people groups' is used in the context of overseas missions, but a similar phenomenon exists in the UK – non-churched groups of people and cultures with little or no connection with the gospel or with church.

Within the Church Growth movement, Dr Ralph Winter has devised terms for three different types of cultural gap that may need to be bridged:

- E1 **Extension Growth**. This involves planting churches among those who don't go to church, but are of an identical culture to the sending church. One example is St Philip's Church in East Kent, started by Holy Trinity, Margate, on a freshly-built middle class housing estate.

- E2 **Bridging Growth 1**. This represents planting among people of related culture. For example, the same Margate parish created 'Harvest New Anglican Church'. This is based on network evangelism and cell life, and meets in a school. Its style meant it was more able to cross English class barriers.[9]

- E3 **Bridging Growth 2**. This is planting in a distanced culture, such as among a different language group, or for adherents of another world religion. An example of this kind of venture is Holy Trinity, Hounslow, which reopened St Paul Hounslow in the early 1990s, sending the vicar and a mixed-race team to try to reach out to its large Asian community.

To state the obvious, the wider the cultural gap being crossed, the greater will be the likely difference between the 'new' and the sending church. The wider the cultural gap to be crossed, the riskier the venture and the more complex is the mental, emotional and ecclesiastical leap that the mission team has to make. As the UK population becomes increasingly post-Christian, so the cultural gap to be crossed in any planting venture will widen.[10] This is the cultural context within which the Church in England now exists, such that missionary cross-cultural training should be an inherent part of ministerial theological education.

important issue: can we justify planting a church for only one sort of people?

The Homogeneous Unit Principle (HUP) is one of the most contentious issues that arise in connection with church planting. The principle was conceived and popularized by the missionary thinker and planter Donald McGavran in his 1955 book *Bridges of God*.[11]

The principle states that: 'People like to become Christians without crossing racial/linguistic/class/cultural barriers.' In other words, they prefer to remain who they are culturally while changing to being Christian. Culturally they remain the same, and tend to gather with others from the same culture who share their faith. It is this sameness that marks the group as 'homogeneous'.

McGavran devised his Homogeneous Unit Principle from observation, principally in India. There the gospel spread across whole people groups (such as the conversion of whole villages) who were evangelized by those from that community. In one sense, he simply said 'this is how the gospel travels most easily'. However, for nearly 50 years, controversy has followed his conclusion. Some are strongly critical of HUP. They argue that the New Testament sees Jesus as reconciler, breaking down barriers between God and human beings, and between human person and human person. So Paul writes to the Galatians: 'There is no longer Jew or Greek, there is no longer slave or free, there is no longer male and female.'[12]

One reply to this concern is to affirm the diversity of creation. God is creator of all, and is also creator of specific and diverse cultures. Whilst elements of all cultures are damaged by the Fall, like the rest of creation, culture is part of God's handiwork.

A second strand is to look at the Incarnation, challenging the church planter to follow Jesus' example of choosing a specific culture and time into which to be born. The incarnation principle points to the planting of churches that are culture-specific for those being reached.

A third factor comes from the theology of Good News for the Oppressed. Sociological study shows that, when two cultures are together in a social context, a healthy heterogeneous mixture does not result – one tends to dominate the other. The culture of those with the educational and economic power tends to come out on top. An attempt at diversity becomes dominance.

Some think that the Church of England's broad failure to express church within the culture of the urban poor is the chief reason why the Anglican Church has seldom effectively reached them. Good news for the poor is only truly good news when it empowers the poor or marginalized to form their own communities of faith, in which indigenous people work together for change and renewal. This resonates with the experience of churches arising out of community projects and of Base Ecclesial Communities.

Thus some aspects of theology point to a culture-specific social expression of the gospel. Other aspects challenge us to build bridges of unity and reconciliation between such groups. The answer may be to accept initial cultural similarity while seeking gradual cultural diversity, expressed in interdependence between groups unlike one another.

is mission about widening choice or increasing access?

One aim through planting is to increase *choice* for people who are not drawn to any existing churches.[13] This could also be planting to increase denominational choice, or it might be planting to increase the choice of ecclesiastical tradition offered by a denomination.

The danger of the latter 'choice' motive is that this is not really a mission reason. Any church can easily become self-satisfied or inward looking, and lead to disunity and less overall effectiveness. However, if the creation of more choice is planned, agreed and amicable, it can provide a better range of churches, which together will suit a wider range of people, including those not yet Christian.

Another planting aim can be to increase *access* – planting more (not different) churches, in order to make church easier to get to. Areas can be cut off from existing church provision by roads, railways or hills. Distances can be too far for convenience. Pram-pushing distance is one good measurement. However, the danger of only increasing access is that more of the same kinds of church may not attract people who presently ignore the existing types.

When the above questions of mission goal are put, then choices about which expression or type of church is suitable begin to have a mission rationale and motivation.

the second dimension: who is the plant *by*?

Having established who an expression of church is for – the mission goal – it is next necessary to become clearer about what sort of team is needed – the mission resource to respond to the mission goal. There are choices to be made about the kind of church into which it is hoped to grow, all subject to an assessment of the mission context.

This dimension might be described as the **height** of the plant. Some sub-questions help to clarify the choices, all of which are different variables.

is the need for progression or pioneer planting?

'Progression planting' describes the progress that can be made by a plant that builds upon the presence of a significant number of existing Christians in a network group or geographical area. It is a way of working that builds on existing strength and contacts. By contrast, 'pioneer planting' is the call for some to plant in places and cultures in which at present there are few, if any, known Christians. Pioneer planting is a way of working by responding to weakness. Clearly both tasks are valid.

The advantages of progression planting are those associated with strength. The team who is already part of the mission context understands it and its culture, and should have a wealth of existing relationships on which to build in evangelism. There are also likely to be sufficient numbers in the team so that the variety of different tasks that are part of becoming a new church can be taken up relatively easily.

The progression task looks easier, but fresh and compelling pioneer contexts are growing in number, needing church planting pioneers to respond.[14] It is important to recognize that pioneer plants are not always cross-cultural – they may simply involve the development of a church in a context where there is currently no church. The lack of existing church people in a context can be due to factors such as large roads or railways, or social trends such as the catchment areas for schools, or presence or absence of shopping centres.

The difference between progression and pioneer planting matters, because they start at different points in terms of local spiritual history, and they involve different resources. Pioneer teams for non-churched people tend to be smaller – partly because they can be difficult to recruit, and partly because large groups might appear to be like an invasion of do-gooders to the present inhabitants. In smaller pioneer teams, the presence of gifted, resilient and visionary people who will work well together is essential. They have the advantage of being more flexible. Large incoming teams face the temptation of setting up and being church in the same way as they experienced church before being sent out, and the venture then fails to engage with local people.[15]

what size of planting unit?
The decision about whether to adopt a cell or congregation model will be partly influenced by the numbers of people that the planting church can afford to give (as well as the number that can be recruited from elsewhere). Experience has shown that the dynamics, challenges and necessary skills are different for different planting unit sizes. There are distinct types of plant that can be categorized according to the size of the starting team.[16] Each has its own advantages, disadvantages and keys to success.[17]

The cultural question needs to be explored – how far will a different form of church be necessary to reach this group? How much distance or space should be made from forms of church they may have known and/or rejected? These questions may lead those working deliberately with the non-churched to conclude that 'congregational' church is not the place to start.

There is some evidence that the contexts listed below particularly benefit from a type of small group church or from incorporating 'small group' into another expression of church.

- Working with non-churched where there is a bad image of church to live down.
- Working with churches arising out of community projects.
- Working with those with addiction problems.
- Working where young disciples need peer group accountability.

is the need for a multiple congregation or to work from another site?
'Multiple congregations' are instances of where a church sustains more than one, relatively distinct, congregation. Many Anglican churches already accept this pattern with their '8.00 Communion' congregation and their main morning congregation, although seldom would this be seen as part of a mission strategy. Multiple congregations motivated by mission are a deliberate attempt to serve a variety of people and their spiritual and cultural needs, providing different ways in which people can explore and express their faith in worship. A church might – for mission purposes – offer an early Sunday morning all-age service, and a later Sunday morning more

reflective or teaching-oriented service, and/or an evening youth or Taizé event. The variety of congregations might include non-Sunday services or events.

The question whether the multiplication (or planting) of congregations within one building is preferable to the planting of church in a different place should flow from the first question above: 'Who is the church plant for?' The answer will have implications for the identity of the emerging church and the kind of mission resources it will need or attract.

Things to be considered include:

- The proposed location and accessibility for the group to be reached.
- The limitations of the size and facilities of existing buildings.
- The image of the chosen venue.
- The cultural messages given by the choice of building.
- Does the 'sent' congregation need to become significantly different from the 'sending' one?

how dependent or mature is this church plant intended to be?

Breaking New Ground helpfully addressed this topic.[18] The vocabulary used to describe a new venture can give strong clues to how that venture is perceived. Those with least independence are simply called 'services'; those with some independence are called 'congregations'; and those with the most independence are recognized as adult 'churches'. The language of 'services' and 'congregations' can betray a worrying attempt to maintain dependency and control. In the past this has led to frustration and failure in traditional church plants. For mission and church health there should be a firm commitment to as adult an interdependence as is possible, as *Breaking New Ground* upheld.

> The healthiest way to foster the sustained onward growth of a church plant is to move as rapidly as possible to an equal partnership with the sponsoring church.[19]

Two fundamental dimensions have so far been explored – 'Who is this plant for?' and 'Who is this plant by?' The third area looks at how partnerships with the wider Church will be forged and sustained.

the third dimension: who is the plant *with*?

This dimension explores both the issue of catholicity, and also an issue that is familiar on the world mission scene: who are the partners in mission for those sent? How are they supported and to whom do they relate and belong? This dimension can be described as the **DEPTH** of the plant. What strength is in reserve?

The history and instincts of the Church of England mean that issues connected with the parish boundary have loomed large in previous considerations of church planting. Territory has been important in order to define responsibility. It has helped fix a sense of belonging and also guaranteed diversity – ensuring that the ethos and traditions of neighbouring Anglican churches are not unfairly eroded by competition or encroachment.

However, concern for parish boundaries needs to be considered in the light of the mission context in which the Church now finds itself. The 'Who with?' question comes third after the 'Who for?' and 'Who by?' questions. In deciding what kind of church plant best suits people outside the Christian faith, it is not appropriate to *begin* with issues about internal parochial organization. Where non-parish-boundary or cross-parish-boundary mission is contemplated, early consultation is to be commended. But the mission imperative needs to flavour and guide those consultations.

Support and partnership are important. Partners make a difference – they give strength in depth, and they are part of the overall nurture of the plant. *Breaking New Ground* suggested four different categories of church plant. Although these categories are often used to label different types of plant, they are, in fact, an attempt to describe some of the relationships with sending church that are possible. They describe how to be mission partners, not the mission goals.

runners

These are so named after the habit of, for example, a strawberry plant, which sends out a shoot nearby. They root and grow a fresh plant and, eventually, the biological link – the runner – withers.[20]

What are 'Runners' like?

- They are started within, and remain within, a parish.[21] There are close links and usually support from the sending church.
- The chosen meeting place falls within the parish. No other Anglican church is directly involved.
- Usually the team that is sent is fewer than 50 people but greater than twelve.
- The process can be easily repeated – as long as there are further definite areas to go to and people willing to be sent.

- When the new plant has established, the runner link from the mother plant naturally withers (although they may remain adjacent).

- The close relational link often creates plants that are very similar to the mother. The ability of runner church planting to create diversity has not been high.

grafts

This biological metaphor follows the practice of introducing a fresh shoot into a slit cut into another stock. The vigour of the new shoot and the sap of the old stock combine to produce a more fruitful specimen.

What are 'Grafts' like?

- With permission they cross a parish, deanery or diocesan boundary, in order to join another existing church, who become their partners. The link to the sending church diminishes.

- Just as with a gardening graft, the incoming team or shoot is smaller than the congregation or stock that receives them. The incoming team usually has a junior role within the receiving church.

- The meeting place is usually the building of the receiving congregation.

- The purpose is to revive the mission emphasis of the new overall congregation. This pattern has often been used with pastoral reorganization schemes.

- The difficult issues are whether this slim resource can revive the larger stock. In addition, the ability to create something new (should that be required) can be limited. Grafts are usually a renewing, not a revolutionary device.[22]

transplants

This is the process of taking a large garden plant, dividing it, and replanting part in a new location, so the parts have space to grow in size.

What are 'Transplants' like?

- Transplants usually cross parish boundaries with permission, to join as partners with another, but struggling, church congregation.

- However, the sent team is usually larger than the receiving church, and – more importantly – the sent team is in the senior partner role.

- Usually the building of the receiving church will be used.

- The size is often 50 or more people.

- The incoming team may retain close relationships with its sending church, and so have some characteristics of the Runner. But the aim from the start is to become an independent parish, so that any dependency link falls away fairly quickly, although links by association may remain.

- The advantage is a 'from strength, in strength' dynamic with more rapid resulting growth. The disadvantage is a tendency to lack flexibility to create something different, should that be advisable. However, if a new step is needed and agreed, resources towards that goal are easily available.[23]

seeds

'Seeds' refer to the process by which a tiny seed is blown on the wind, perhaps a long way away from its host – both in terms of distance and environment – and may make a new beginning where perhaps this kind of plant was previously absent.

What are 'Seeds' like?

- Seeds cross boundaries perhaps more freely than any other group. Their mission partners are furthest away, rather like missionaries to foreign lands with mission societies back home who pray and support, but cannot be with them physically.
- By definition, seeds are a small group of highly motivated and possibly highly skilled people. They are from one to six people at most.
- People on seed teams move their home in order to plant, so that they can identify more deeply with the area to which they are called.[24] They may even have been brought together from different sources to form the team.
- The great advantage is they best exemplify the planting missionary dynamic of dying to their previous identity in order to reincarnate the gospel and church in the mission context.
- If the seeds are small in number, then the years taken to make a significant difference can be considerable. Ways to recruit, train, deploy and support seed teams – or missionary communities – have exercised church planters in England for years.[25]

a summary

Good planting methodology asks three questions, in this order:

- Who is the mission *for?* – mission *goal* questions
- Who is the mission *by?* – mission *resource* questions
- Who is the mission *with?* – mission *partner* questions.

What is important is to:

- Keep the three questions separate at their own stage.
- Explore what is appropriate to that question.
- Choose the way forward that actually suits the factors that are present in the situation.
- Ensure that mission-questions drive the church-answers, not vice versa.

Those who start with questions about the relationship to the existing church have already made the most common and most dangerous mistake.

Start with the Church and the mission will probably get lost. Start with mission and it is likely that the Church will be found.

A story . . . of a church with three deceivingly simple questions
St Saviour's, Washington DC is now over 30 years old. It exists outside the government buildings area, in a city of urban poverty and high ethnic mix. The church has nine separate congregations, each with its own ethos. At present each congregation offers a speciality, for example, a hospital for street people, a job centre, a housing association, a coffee shop and book centre, and an intergenerational home caring for the elderly.

A person coming off the streets might move through the ministries offered by various congregations. They are united through the work of the teaching and discipleship programme put on by the Servant Leadership School – the focus of another of the congregations.

The church explores three questions when working towards setting up another congregation.

What is the mission to this area?

What kind of community is needed to sustain the mission?

What set of spiritual disciplines is required to sustain the community in that mission?[26]

patterns of worship

If authorized church plants and fresh expressions of church within the Church of England are to bear an Anglican 'family likeness' then that will be evident in various ways in their corporate worship.

Common Worship: Lent, Holy Week and Easter; The Promise of His Glory; and, in particular, the resources and guidelines offered in *New Patterns for Worship*, provide a rich resource.

However, these may not prove sufficient. The Archbishops' Council's 'National Youth Strategy' has already acknowledged the need to identify good practice and provide resource materials for youth worship. Many fresh expressions of church give particular emphasis to small groups or cells, and need appropriate material for that setting. Alternative worship congregations, in particular, have proved to be a rich source of liturgical creativity, combining the contemporary and the ancient in new ways. 'Table church' has created a liturgy around a meal.

This report affirms the importance of a culturally appropriate Anglicanism emerging 'from below' – from the interaction between an Anglican planting team, the target culture and the historic gospel. This has implications for the process that shapes decisions about corporate worship.

Underlying *Common Worship* was a 'new strategy'.[27] It focused on identifying a 'common core' of the Church's worship. The core was not to be regarded as static, although some elements – in particular, eucharistic prayers – needed full authorization. The core was seen to be evolving and was, in part, to be shaped by cultural circumstances.

This balance between loyalty to our liturgical inheritance (together with the doctrinal safeguarding of key texts like eucharistic prayers) and appropriateness to cultural context expresses in microcosm the challenge of cross-cultural church planting, and the tension between relevance and syncretism.

The 'common core' strategy underlying *Common Worship* is helpful. It emphasizes patterns and structures instead of giving detailed and prescribed texts. If church planters are trained in the overall structures and patterns of Christian worship, then they should be trusted with the freedom, together with their new congregations, to develop culturally appropriate liturgy from below. This approach will help discourage the cloning of patterns of liturgy and of church in new areas of mission.

church planting in rural areas

Church planting in rural areas seldom involves a 'traditional church plant' with a new building. Buildings are generally not in short supply. Perhaps not surprisingly one response to the survey of dioceses in 2002 was 'with 648 churches in this diocese, there is little incentive to plant more'. Anglican ministry in the English countryside is frequently characterized by the 'multi-parish benefice' in which each village, however tiny, has its own parish church – sharing its vicar with neighbouring parishes.

It is not that more church buildings are needed. What is needed are fresh expressions of church that can relate to rural dwellers who do not connect with the current ministry of their village church. Although traditional expressions of church have retained more cultural relevance in the countryside than in urban areas, social change is well under way. Rural churches with inherited patterns are frequently failing to reach the younger generation. Many village communities have undergone upheaval, as local young people are forced to find affordable housing in towns and are replaced by more affluent commuters. Hence 'urban' factors such as network-living, choice and mobility are now strongly present in the rural scene. Any of the fresh expressions of church listed in Chapter 8 might have a 'rural version', apart from the 'traditional' church plant.

A story: Warham, Winchester Diocese

In the mid-1980s the owner of a manor house in rural Hampshire invited Holy Trinity Brompton to run an Alpha course for his neighbours and friends. Many became Christians or engaged with their faith in a more committed way. That group then wanted their contacts and friends to experience Alpha, and over a decade at least 200 people's lives were affected.

The area is one where a 'next door neighbour' may be five miles away. The Diocese of Winchester authorized a redundant hamlet church as a centre for midweek training and monthly Sunday services, whilst the growing network was also encouraged to be involved with local parishes.

In 1997, Tim Humphrey was appointed as 'Faith Development Officer' for the north of the diocese, and as 'Warham Missioner' formally to lead the group. In the following five years a Warham Community was established, from which trained teams resourced dozens of Alpha courses focused in some ten parishes. Community members and converts were organized in dispersed cells across a 20-mile radius, and grouped into three regions for periodic celebrations and Alpha services. This fresh expression of church is in the process of gaining Extra Parochial Place (EPP) status.

Fresh expressions of church in the countryside tend to start by reaching networks of mobile people over a larger geographical area than the single parish. Sometimes this is mission led, as with a youth congregation working across all the parishes of a high school's catchment area. Sometimes, it is more to do with scarcity of leadership. Few church planters are placed in rural parishes. In a multi-parish benefice, clergy and readers will be already ministering in half a dozen or more separate congregations and cannot sustain new initiatives in each parish.

Because church planting in rural areas almost always involves growing a new expression of church alongside the old, sensitivity is particularly needed towards the relationship between fresh expressions of church and small parish churches who could see the innovation as 'competition'. However, small congregations may welcome a fresh expression of church if it serves a clearly different part of the community, releasing the congregation from the pressure to change a dearly held worship style or to attempt the impossible task of meeting the diversifying needs of everyone. The pressure of responding to variety is often increased because, in the countryside, the Church of England may be the only visible Christian presence. Therefore, many Anglican congregations contain high numbers of Christians originally from other denominations. That diversity can be a source of tension, but it can also be a benefit, in that it means that planting teams are likely to contain a denominational mix, and a variety of insight and approach.

A story: '4 All', Southrepps, Trunch Team Ministry

When the Revd David Bartlett became Southrepps Team Vicar, he intended to heed the bishop's advice not to change anything for a year. However, it soon became apparent that about 20 Christians from different parishes had an unmet need for contemporary worship in which their children would happily share. Some of these families had started to give up on existing church.

It was decided to start a service at 4.30 p.m., when it would not conflict with other services in the team and would

> *complement the existing monthly 'Open Doors' children's club,*
> *held at that time. The style was informal, interactive and*
> *ended with a shared tea. Adults who attended '4 All' were*
> *invited to an Alpha course or to join a cell. Just over a year*
> *after its start, 70 people were involved on a regular basis.*
> *'4 All' simultaneously strengthened the commitment of*
> *existing congregation members and attracted new people*
> *who would never attend a more traditional service.*

Two issues, common in Church of England rural ministry, can either offer great potential or danger to fresh expressions of church.

The first is the multi-parish benefice. A united benefice with six parochially-based churches who relate to one another as sister churches has a ready-made framework for recognizing as fully church a new church based on cell or network. It would be a partner in the gospel with a mission that complements the group or team. The danger is that, in benefices where each parish church has its own PCC, fresh expressions of church will not have a suitable mechanism for accountability. Nor can they easily find an equal place alongside older forms of church, including responsibility for finances and payment of parish share. A single PCC for the whole benefice, with DCCs for individual churches old and new, would be a more sympathetic structure in which fresh expressions of church can be accountable, nurtured and mature.

The second issue is that of church buildings. Ancient hallowed buildings can be wonderful centres for worship. However, churches in the countryside struggle to subsidize the conservation of the nation's heritage to the extent that they have in past years. It is important that they are able to consider first the mission to which God has called them. Where there are excessive numbers of such buildings in small populations and cost or conservation interests put adaptation for modern needs out of reach, they starve mission and the development of fresh expressions of church by taking a disproportionate share of money, time and effort. How these two issues are addressed is vital to the future of planting fresh expressions of church in the countryside.

working for maturity

The necessity of, and the path to, maturity for fresh expressions of church has already been shaped by great mission thinkers of the past such as Henry Venn of the Church Missionary Society.[28] He was one of a few notable people to campaign for the deliberate foundation of indigenous churches that fitted the culture and were led by local people.

By 1846 Venn spoke of 'introducing a self-supporting principle into the Native Churches'. This developed and is now remembered as the 'Three Self' formula: self-supporting, self-governing and self-extending, or sometimes 'self-propagating'. These categories help describe three dimensions of church maturity.

The same pattern is appropriate for today's church planting. This is especially true of fresh expressions of church, as they may be particularly vulnerable and constrained by limitations on the placing of full-time staff and external financial support. Henry Venn's principles are a good framework of understanding for both sender and sent churches. They are a practical way to measure degrees of interdependence, and should be considered by church plants, fresh expressions of church and dioceses.

the 'three self' principles

Planned progress to self-government is vital for church plants and fresh expressions of church. Self-government will be enabled or frustrated by the ability to be self-financing, and healthiness will be tested by fruitfulness of self-propagation.

self-propagating

Stories of planted churches becoming, in their turn, wise sending churches of further fresh expressions of church are causes for joy. All expressions of church, new or old, should include the potential for reproduction.

Any growing church will be committed to developing gifts and ministries among its members. Raising the next generation of leaders is a good test of any local church, although in some deprived areas this is one of the hardest challenges. The commitment to propagation should be inherent in the thinking of the plant's leadership and membership. This commitment helps them to continue to face outwards and sustain an attitude of giving to others.

self-financing

Visibility of costs and accounts will help plants in relationship to their parochial sending church and to the diocese. Visibility means honesty and trust, and leads to better decisions. Visibility means honesty about the costs of running a fresh expression of church, and about any subsidies and support that enable the church to continue.

- In the planning stage, it is recommended to set and agree a budget for the new church. This includes:

  ○ Salary costs

  ○ Housing costs

  ○ Buildings costs

  ○ Equipment costs

  ○ Training costs

  ○ Evangelistic costs.

Consultants find most discussion about church planting tends to revolve around the third and fourth items. Compared to the first and second items, these represent small amounts. The third and fourth may only be £100s per annum, whereas the first two can easily run to £30,000 annually (not including any capital costs of housing). The fifth and sixth areas are important, because developing gifts and ministries is direct linkage into being self-propagating, and to be in mission is why the plant was started in the first place.

- A budget in outline for several years ahead should be agreed, to determine what subsidy may be needed.

Total costs for a year can easily be £35,000 if full-time paid leaders are involved. If an old church building is inherited this may also need significant levels of expenditure. Fresh expressions of church often have commendably high levels of fringe members, or of those beginning to discover Christian discipleship. Dioceses will probably need to enter into an arrangement for a diminishing subsidy, and/or relief from diocesan share arrangements.

self-governing

All church plants and fresh expressions of church benefit from the process of learning to run their own affairs, as far as they are able. Learning to make decisions and taking responsibility (including permission to fail) are part of growth and maturity. Protective 'sending' churches need to discover how to give away control and power, and celebrate the independence and interdependence of the new church.[29]

In 1994, *Breaking New Ground* grasped and advocated this same point:

It is apparent that the more the parent churches share power and place trust in the plant, the more vigorous the growth in quality and quantity that results.[30, 31]

Such self-governance does not mean that the local church has no links with other churches. Rather there is interdependence of churches within a deanery and diocese, with accountability to bishop and synod. Good practice commends the granting of appropriate legal status to fresh expressions of church.

Within Anglicanism, legal status and forms of self-government are closely linked. It is beyond the scope of this report to recommend detailed legislative proposals. This report will make a number of general recommendations in Chapter 8.

why does legal status for plants and fresh expressions of church matter?

- It can be compared to having a spine in the body. This is often invisible to the casual glance, but most of the other visible realities hang off it and, if it goes seriously wrong, major handicap results. Lack of legal existence can make a plant collapse at a time of stress and, if present, can help support it through crisis.

- Legal status is protection against the possible negative impact of shifts of personality or policy within a diocese or the 'sending' church. It ensures that a young church is properly recognized and respected.

- Young churches that exist only by grace and favour can develop financial obligations to the diocese, but no legal rights from the diocese. Responsibilities and rights should go together.

- Evangelistic enthusiasm in a young church, and even rising numbers of attenders, may not guarantee a church plant's future. This is particularly true in the distribution of leadership resources – vigour has been used as an argument for a church plant *not* to need a leader. Where a plant remains 'an interesting experiment' there is equal freedom to praise it or to close it.

The above is not an argument for all expressions of church to be made parishes. In many cases that would be neither wanted nor appropriate. However, for fresh expressions of church to be simply designated as 'experiments' or 'projects' is both dangerous and insulting.

When so-called 'emerging church' is typically reduced to a 'project' that gets done, rather than a fundamental theology/philosophy/approach, it is being marginalized. The challenge to the whole Church is to find ways by which planting concepts and insights can become embedded and normative, rather than added on to its life.

Methods of validating fresh expressions of church are needed.[32] Chapter 8 explores at some length what these might be. Other criteria from *Breaking New Ground* have been in circulation for nearly ten years. Yet there is still considerable resistance in practice to giving church plants and fresh expressions of church the right to Anglican citizenship. In a few cases the process of acceptance and recognition has been so reluctant and slow that valuable resources to the Church of England have been lost.[33]

To show church plants and expressions that they belong, by positive legal inclusion, strengthens the bonds between new and old. It affirms the welcomed diversity demonstrated by the range from traditional to radical. It will place emerging and existing in a framework for ongoing conversation and mutual learning. In short, it treats legally what theologically ought to be one body – one body with different parts, each valuing the other, by their identity under a common head in Christ.

some questions for discussion

➤ Have we imposed models of church on people who don't want them? (Bible suggestion: Ephesians 4.11-16.)

➤ In the area where you live (rural, urban, suburban) – or the network in which you live – what fresh expressions of church might realistically be developed that could relate to people who are not currently in contact with church?

➤ What attributes make a local church 'mature'? What are the characteristics of any mature churches in your area? Can a church ever be *too* mature?!

➤ This chapter talks about creative use of liturgy. What elements of your worship can aid mission in your local context? What aspects of liturgy and worship services could hinder mission?

➤ This chapter suggests that the following is wisely observed:

Start with the Church and the mission will probably get lost.
Start with mission and it is likely that the Church will be found.

What would it mean – in practice – to 'start with mission', and not 'start with the Church'?

chapter 7

an enabling framework for a missionary church

Ten years ago *Breaking New Ground* expressed a hope.

> We need to find ways to enable diverse styles of church life to co-exist without always having recourse to territorial or even denominational boundaries. And here the church planting movement has much to teach us. Further, an Episcopal church is well placed to discern when, in order to be rooted in the community, the focus on parochial territory needs supplementing with a realistic awareness of network and neighbourhood . . . in such situations the assertion that the parish boundaries are paramount will merely paralyse initiative.[1]

The time has come to turn these aspirations into practicalities, and four significant issues will be discussed in this chapter.

what will work for networks?

Since *Breaking New Ground* the Church of England has seen the slow emergence of non-territorial network churches.[2] This trickle is now beginning to flow faster. Following precedents set in Sheffield and Canterbury dioceses, at present about half of those network churches have obtained Extra Parochial Place (EPP) status, nearly always through protracted periods of negotiation and via the good offices of a sympathetic ear within an episcopal staff team. The remaining network churches have been either actively discouraged from taking this route, or they have applied for it and have been turned down by the sending parish or diocese.

The Group reviewing the 1983 Pastoral Measure, concludes in its questionnaire of January 2003:

> Current provisions, including those for setting up extra parochial places, are not always wholly satisfactory or appropriate, involving as they do the use of procedures and structures not intended to deal with modern forms of 'networked' non-territorial churches. We believe new provision is needed for use on a permissive basis to allow recognition

and encouragement to be given to non-parochial church and mission models.

These words are welcome. They make clear that 'network' is becoming a significant way in which English society now functions and that many of the fresh expressions of church and existing church plants are churches working within the reality of network. This is not a provision for the unusual within the normal. This is coming to terms with a future norm that is already apparent in the present.

> There is a fabric of the old way of being society and being church. We are not about patching the fabric of that old garment but seeking to set up a new loom to weave the new fabric for tomorrow's society of the kingdom.

how can existing plants become recognized 'adult' churches?

There has been a long history of new congregations being kept in a dependent state, in which their maturity has been implicitly or explicitly questioned. The word 'adult' in the above heading is used to make clear the status of a fresh expression of church in relation to other surrounding Anglican churches. 'Adult' does not imply that members of the church are all of 'adult' age. 'Adult' churches are those that are fully recognized, respected and cherished by other churches that have a longer history. Their length of existence or style of worship or community are not factors that diminish how the fresh expression is viewed or treated.

Chapter 6 of this report argues that general mission thinking, and the specific recommendations of *Breaking New Ground* in particular, underline the importance of adult recognition for church plants and fresh expressions. There are many stories of plants being kept in a position of financial dependency, and lacking synodical rights or legal status (or being kept in a subordinate position). The national Church should be concerned to ensure that fresh expressions and plants should really be church, and should encourage all attempts to gain recognition and full involvement with the structures and life of the wider Church.

Some have argued that there may be untapped scope for leadership authorization within existing regulations governing the licensing of the leader of a fresh expression of church. This may bring flexibility to the start of a process, but it does not address the question of the status of the church that is formed as a result, nor say much about its responsibilities and rights in relationship with other parishes or a diocese.

recovering existing guidance and good practice

Appendix One in *Breaking New Ground* contains guidelines that offer a staged process of transition to maturity and legal recognition for church plants. The guidelines cover plants starting from different strengths and sizes, and taking different lengths of time to become sustainable and 'adult'. It was, perhaps, a mistake to relegate them to an appendix in *Breaking New Ground*, where they have remained invisible to the wider Church. The guidelines have not featured in broad diocesan planning, and have not been taken into the training offered to new incumbents. This omission should be reversed, and active use should be made of what is already published and approved by General Synod in *Breaking New Ground*.

how well do present legal options work for the range of church plants and fresh expressions?

This review of present legal options is based on 20 years of church planting experience. This section covers how progress toward maturity and recognition works under the existing legislation, and the advantages and disadvantages of each option, as well as how likely it is that a new form of church can gain this status. What is presented is a summary, not a closely argued case.[3]

Legal Option	Description	Advantages	Disadvantages	Summary
Parish status (new church building)	The church is given a physical territory, like other existing churches in the diocese.	Succession of ordained leadership. Housing for church leader. Self-governing PCC. Synodical voting rights. A building as a focus. Instant recognition from other churches.	Very difficult to obtain. Area needs population of over 5,000. Costs of building church and house.	Parish status ensures the church's place within the diocese. Unsuitable for network churches, but suits geographic plants.

Legal Option	Description	Advantages	Disadvantages	Summary
Parish status (existing church building)	A new congregation takes on a closing or redundant church.	As above.	History of decline to turn around. Boundaries may not match the mission task. Care for parish may not fit with a church serving a specialist culture like youth.	As above.
The Conventional District	A temporary quasi-parish is made out of an area of one or more existing adjacent parishes. By convention the area is designated as a district – hence the name.	An ordained leader (but without freehold). A Church Council with some independence. Synodical voting rights.	Its continued existence depends on the goodwill of the incumbent, who may change. Ministers usually stay for a shorter time than an incumbent with freehold. Building less of a focus than the parish church. Slow pace to becoming a full parish. Not suitable for network, since area based.	A stepping stone to parish status, but vulnerable to leadership change. Only useful as part of a longer-term plan to achieve parish status for a new church serving a specific area.
The Proprietary Chapel	A chapel independent of local structures, used in past centuries to accommodate different traditions.		Often an adversarial history. No mission focus.	Rarely used due to its adversarial history.
Team ministry	Usually three or more churches and congregations made into a team, serving a united area. One leader is team rector.	Puts a church plant within a wider family. Some security in early years. Team vicars have longer licences than curates. A further plant can easily join the widening team.	Team rector can control ministry appointments. Complex structures can add burdens to a young church. The church plant may not be given synodical voting rights. Some poor experiences of teams, leading to some being disbanded.	Church plants in teams can remain as junior partners, without automatic synodical rights, and quota responsibilities. This prevents them gaining 'adult' status.

Legal Option	Description	Advantages	Disadvantages	Summary
			Little training to help clergy work in teams. Development of plant into a fuller identity beyond the team is rare. Cumbersome to set up.	
Group ministry	A set of parishes retain their own PCC, but treat their territory as common.	Local ministers agree their level of mutual support. Agreed flexibility within group. A network church can exist within the area of the group. Retains diverse traditions, while building unity. Each church has self-government, with synodical voting rights.	Vulnerable to change of incumbents. Area of group may not match the spread of the network.	More promising than a team, in terms of flexibility for mission, and gaining clear identity within the wider Church. They may be easier to set up than teams. Good for a town where networks are likely to be mainly within the town, but may not be the answer in a city, or rural situation.
Extra Parochial Place (EPP)	A building that is the focus of a special ministry, such as a retreat centre or an army chapel.	Gives network churches a right to exist. Succession of ministry probable. Self-governing. The church is clearly seen as distinct from parish church.	Long process to gain this status. Hard to give to a church that meets in more than one place, e.g. cell church. No synodical rights. Minister can be limited to pastoral care of only existing members (Canon C8).	A helpful legal recognition of certain networked Christian communities. Synodical rights and quota responsibilities need to be further explored.
Church plants as Local Ecumenical Partnerships (LEP)	The new plant is started by more than one denomination.	Good for areas of large-scale new housing. Spreads costs among denominations. Impression of churches working together is good for mission.	More church structures to relate to. Still need to work out Anglican relationships, whether team, group, parish. Can get focused on ecumenism, and not on mission.	LEP church plants have had a mixed record. A light touch as far as relating to the various denominations may be needed, without losing identity within the wider Church.

what is needed now?

resourcing a planting movement

Across the denominations, the last 20 years have seen creative developments in mission and church planting. However, the dynamic of a church planting movement has never been released. There are several reasons for this:

- The parish system is well designed to allow a fresh expression of church within its borders. But the parish system is not well designed to foster fresh expressions or church plants if they cross borders.

- Permission to reopen redundant churches or to rescue terminally ill parishes is difficult to seek and hard to secure.

- Few parishes are large enough to sustain multiplication, and most large churches are unable to persuade their dioceses to allow them to recruit the number of full-time staff – even if lay – that would be needed.

- Neither pioneer nor entrepreneur leaders find life within Anglicanism easy. There is neither a vocational structure, nor support for them.

- Anecdotal evidence suggests that many leaders oversee the start of a creative and contextual expression of church, but then find themselves in different roles for their next job. Their skills and experience are not used again, nor passed on to other suitable candidates.

Even a vigorous Anglican multiplication movement from Holy Trinity, Brompton in partnership with the Diocese of London has led to only fifteen planted churches in as many years. Furthermore, the HTB family tree reveals[4] that only four of the fifteen have themselves further reproduced.

St Thomas in Sheffield (an Anglican-Baptist Local Ecumenical Partnership) has been encouraged to work across the city on church planting mission for the past eight years. Implementing an element of diocesan strategy, they adopted a 'Resource Church' model[5] to support a movement of both network and neighbourhood church, currently comprising 29 clusters (missionary communities). These are grouped into eight celebrations that gather around a shared mission vision such as students, the workplace, youth inner urban estates, young adults and the parish neighbourhood of Crookes in Sheffield.

Wherever a resource church is capable of multiplying church plants as an agreed component of diocesan strategy, it should be encouraged to do so, but by itself, this is nowhere near enough to meet the scale of the challenge we face.

is a new missionary Order needed?

A new legal category of 'Bishop's Order' may begin to open the way to creating what is needed in terms of nurturing, validating and multiplying fresh expressions of church, without making them subject to the existing legislation.[6] A Bishop's Order is accountable and preserves episcopal authority, but growth and resourcing can be encouraged.

new 'Orders'

Within the Diocese of Monmouth, the then Bishop Rowan Williams gave recognition and patronage to two different orders, Jacob's Well (for the ministry of healing) and Living Proof (for community youth work among the non-churched). Episcopal recognition placed both in the overall life of the Church in Wales, but freed them from quasi-parochial status and modelled creative untidiness in church life.[7]

oversight

Like historic Orders, the new Orders need accountable relationship to the bishop. Links to the bishop should be lightweight, yet historically recognizable. This could be an appropriate model for network-based churches, notably Alternative Worship, some cell churches, monastic intentional communities and youth congregations. The problem is that the sheer variety and number could overwhelm the capacity of the present number of bishops to bring effective oversight to them.

Others have wondered whether the growth of network-based churches should lead to the creation of deanery chapters for them in each diocese where they exist. While mutual support, common spiritual reflection and joint strategy all commend themselves, the danger is that this would break both the tie to other clergy, and the complementarity existing between inherited and fresh expressions of church. Occasional meetings such as an annual diocesan day for all church plants and fresh expressions of church might be a better way forward.

finding new levers for change

This report[8] highlights a problem in Anglican methodology. We are an English Church moulded by history and culture to be like the English:

in favour of slow evolutionary change. However, that is not the context we face. At present we do not possess the levers that can accelerate the process of mission response to the changing culture of England.

At the same time, a number of pioneers are living with a tension between the call to be Anglican and the call to be apostolic. They love the Church that nurtured them. They are called to love the world outside it. At best this tension is constructive, with mission and order in dynamic balance. At worst it becomes impossible to maintain.

How can we enable fresh expressions of church to flourish, while being true to what is good in our current systems? Fresh expressions may reach some for Christ, but there is still an important role for the parish where a culture is neighbourhood based, particularly among the less mobile or marginalized in our society, whether rural or urban. Yet the Spirit is bringing forth fresh expressions of church that are connecting with and embodying the changing culture. The underlying conviction of this report is that in the theory and practice of fresh expressions of church and of church planting there are valid lessons for the whole Church. The Church should learn from its growing edges.

appropriate local leadership

This report has identified a variety of principles for church planting and other missionary expressions of church. It has also identified key lessons from recent experience. No one practical factor has greater influence than the quality of leadership.

Some church plants or fresh expressions are primarily the work of individual pioneers. The initial development and sometimes the original vision came from leaders with a God-given entrepreneurial ability in mission. Church Army evangelists, among others, have been released in this way to develop new projects. One such example is Sanctus 1, in central Manchester. The Church needs discernment and authorizing procedures that can recognize and release such pioneers within appropriate frameworks of accountability.

> ### A story: Sanctus 1 in the city centre of Manchester
> *Sanctus 1 is for the city centre residential community and for city centre users. The majority of the people attending are young adults who are exploring the Christian faith within a postmodern world view. It began after a review of mission and ministry in Manchester city centre by the archdeacon, with a*

conclusion that patterns of worship with relevance to younger people should be developed.

In July 2001, Church Army evangelist Ben Edson was appointed as City Centre Missioner, to help create a fresh expression of church for people engaged in a journey of creative exploration into faith, worship, evangelism, friendship and lifestyle.

Ben initially met with four committed Christians who had not found a church. In January 2002 they held their first public act of worship at Manchester Cathedral, attended by 20 people, and leading to setting up a monthly public worship service. The core community, who meet on a Wednesday night, has grown to 22 with a fringe of four or five others. They meet for discussion, worship and friendship.

Public worship services have attracted between 14 and 50 people, and use a DJ playing contemporary secular music, as well as using video and art. The aim is to provide a sacred space in the midst of a busy city.

Sanctus 1 has generated a number of insights, in particular that new creative churches need to re-imagine mission, worship and community, and that fluid structures are needed to facilitate long-term sustainability and adaptability.

However, if pioneers are to establish work that endures, they quickly need to become team leaders. Many new initiatives properly begin with a team, and the capacity to lead and develop a team is crucial. There can be a tension between the visionary and the relational, team-building elements of leadership. Both elements are essential if the work is to last beyond an initial burst of enthusiasm.

Team members should be encouraged to grow in their particular giftings. Ideally, teams should contain members with abilities that the leader lacks, and who can outperform the leader in their areas of gifting. This requires leaders who are secure and know themselves, and it makes for a strong and durable team. Some models of church – like cell church – have an inbuilt procedure for the growth of leaders. But all church plants and fresh expressions need to have the development of leadership as a core part of their DNA.

Team leaders need to develop skills as mentors and trainers. A critical factor that decides whether a new development will be culturally authentic is whether new members are drawn into ministry. The 'planting' team should begin to share power with those they are seeking to reach, at an early stage. Training or coaching involves the empowerment of one person by another through teaching skills and releasing the novice to use them. Mentoring can imply a much deeper process in which, in a trusting relationship, character issues are addressed and underlying principles learned, equipping the mentored to take initiatives that the mentor may not be capable of. Wherever church planting and fresh expressions of church are cross-cultural this is essential, and is a key strategy to ensure inculturation.

second generation

A number of plants and projects have failed or been severely weakened by inappropriate appointments when the pioneer leader has left. Second generation leadership is crucial to long-term health. When a new parish priest is appointed attention is given to the tradition and wishes of the parish with the vacancy, although, once appointed, a new priest is expected to bring new vision. This is a particularly delicate balance when it comes to the appointment of the second-generation leader of a church plant. A domineering style of leadership is usually disastrous. Particular attention needs to be given to the original vision, and to the developing style and ethos of the plant or project. The next leader should be appointed to enrich the vision, not to lead the work in a different direction.

It will often be the case that a new leader should be recruited from outside. However, more consideration should be given to the possibility of the next leader emerging from the established team and, as necessary, being given further training in context.

training

Priority attention needs to be given by the Church of England to the identification and training of leaders for pioneering missionary projects. The possibility of a call to such work needs to be specifically identified in the vocational process. Just as potential theological educators are identified during the selection process, so potential missionary leaders should be identified among ordinands and trainee Church Army evangelists. A course, college or other institution with specialist training skills should be identified within each region, to provide key training modules. Similarly, training curacies and similar key first posts should be provided with proven leaders of church plants and fresh expressions of church. It is then important that they are not pressed into becoming ministers of existing churches, but are deployed in pioneering contexts.

So far in this section attention has been given to ordained or similarly trained and authorized leadership. But, if the missionary challenge we face is to be met, many new initiatives will be lay led. They are also as likely to have emerged unplanned through local discernment of the mission of God, as to have been meticulously planned in advance. This raises new challenges for the discernment, training, recognition and authorization of leaders.

Many dioceses now have a strategy for local ministry with some combination of Ministry Leadership Teams, Readers, NSMs, OLMs, and various forms of authorized lay ministry (evangelists, pastoral assistants, etc.). Ministry emerges 'from below', and the role of stipendiary priests changes towards providing team leadership and equipping team members. This is precisely the strategy that can be extended to church plants and fresh expressions of church.

The critical factor will be our ability to identify and train emerging leaders in context. Our Anglican norm for church leadership has been to distinguish between ordained and lay leadership, to withdraw ordinands from frontline ministry, and then to ordain them after training. This pattern has already been varied by mixed-mode training and by various OLM schemes. Both of these arrangements could provide key elements for a further model. The Church of England will need to develop procedures that provisionally acknowledge lay leaders who are already in place, and then provide training as part of a process of discernment about the appropriate level of medium-term or permanent authorization (Authorized Lay Minister, Reader, OLM, NSM, etc.). The effectiveness of our ministry and mission in the future will depend on our ability to identify, train and authorize 'local' ministers.

bishops in mission

The role of the bishop as leader in mission is crucial to these developments. In harmony with the Pastoral Measure Review Group, this Report recommends revised legal frameworks that include a simple measure empowering bishops to authorize church planting and other strategic mission initiatives.

This is in line with other pressures to ensure that bishops are sufficiently free from administrative overload to be able to invest time in a more apostolic role, developing mission strategy and taking the lead in the discernment of priority mission initiatives.

Bishops have a key role in setting mission priorities, in releasing resources for mission, and in their powers to ordain and license. This includes the ability to send fresh apostolic teams to cultures or areas where the mission presence is thin or non-existent. In connection with this, the Church should note those who are exploring the idea of missionary Orders. Others such as the Church Mission Society and Church Army are exploring the idea of sending teams to relocate to needy areas.

The role of the bishop in brokering new initiatives is addressed later in this chapter in the section 'How do we hold all this together?'

the strategic role of deaneries

In Chapter 1 we identified the increasing influence of 'networks' on the shape of community. Networks have not replaced locality, but they have changed the way we think of ourselves and live our life. In particular, a more mobile society has enlarged the amount of territory across which people regularly travel and within which they forge their identity.

This may give much greater strategic significance to the deanery. Deaneries have the potential to bring together a range of human and financial resources, to consider mission beyond parish boundaries, and to share prayer and encouragement. Canterbury, for example, has delegated to its deaneries the internal apportionment of parish share, strategic decisions about the deployment of full-time clergy and requires from each deanery a mission plan that relates to the Strategic Local Partnership and local authority plan, to ecumenical partnerships and proposed new developments and potential church plants.

As they now stand, not every deanery would be an obvious place for a strategic partnership in mission. History and personalities can make a significant impact on where a deanery places its priorities, and whether it primarily has an administrative or missionary function. Many parishes and benefices have little sense of the deanery at all. However, few parishes can survive alone and none should have to. Once the need of a network approach is recognized, the deanery becomes an essential unit for mission and the role of the area/rural dean and lay chair central to mission planning.

The social context of deaneries is important. If the deanery boundary corresponds well to a town and surrounding villages, or where it exists closely parallel to local government boundaries, it is likely to be a valuable tool for mission planning. London Diocese has organized its deaneries to reflect local government boundaries.

If a deanery does not make sense socially or geographically within its wider community, then there is a strong case for the revision of boundaries. It will be unusual for a deanery to coincide with all of the major boundaries and networks in each area. So mission planning may also have to involve larger units and partnerships. For example, if a youth congregation is planned, then secondary school catchment areas may well prove more important than either parish or deanery boundaries. A partnership between part or all of two or more deaneries may be needed.

Where a city and whole diocese are coterminous, and/or deanery boundaries are more arbitrary and difficult to change, it may make more sense for diocesan strategy to view the whole diocese as its basic unit of mission. In all cases, communicating vision, gaining ownership by the appropriate-sized grouping, and resourcing it to respond to need and opportunity will be necessary.

national, regional and diocesan-wide solutions

Individual parishes are not well placed to look at larger unit sizes and the impact of social trends and population movements. These are appropriate responsibilities for national, regional and diocesan authorities.

Current government proposals plan to increase housing stock by 20 per cent by 2016, with over half of that increase in the south-east of England. This offers a major challenge and opportunity to the Church in England. Large new areas of housing invite strategic fresh expressions of church, as well as the development of the existing worshipping congregations in the places where new housing will be built.

Most major cities are seeing the creation of thousands of city-centre flats to repopulate brownfield sites. The *Tomorrow Project* predicts that the number of single person households is due to grow from 25 per cent in 1991 to 35 per cent by 2016.[9] In all these cases, population movements are a classic opportunity for new churches, as people new to an area are more open to make friends and to explore faith.

These macro shifts in the population require strategic national, regional and diocesan thinking and resourcing, in order for the Church of England to meet the challenge, and to sustain a pattern of being a Church that seeks to connect with all people, whether they identify themselves through their networks or their neighbourhoods.

how do we hold all this together?

Our Anglican identity includes a calling to be a Church for the nation. This mission orientation means that we seek to relate to society as it is (not as we might like it to be) and need continually to assess whether our organizational structures best serve the Church's missionary calling. In 1994, *Breaking New Ground* urged the Church to recognize the complementary realities of parish, neighbourhood and network. Today we can still think 'local', but this may not be the same as 'parochial'.

At diocesan level, four principles may guide the response to new mission opportunities:

- In any proposed mission where new churches beyond parish boundaries are in view, it is both right and necessary that the bishop act as the broker in discussions, with the ability to authorize a new venture or to deny it permission to proceed.
- Proposed fresh expressions of church need to work in ways that are complementary to inherited ways.
- Existing ecclesiastical legal boundaries should be seen as permeable.
- An agreed process is needed to make these values credible.

in any proposed mission where new churches beyond parish boundaries are in view, it is both right and necessary that the bishop act as the broker in discussions
The word 'broker' describes only part of the bishop's role; that of overseeing negotiations with the different parties involved in or affected by the proposal. Within the Church of England, the bishop shares the 'cure of souls' with each priest, licensed lay worker and parish involved, and is the key authority in any renegotiation or development of that 'cure'.

The bishop must have genuine freedom either to authorize a venture, or to deny it permission to proceed, through his authority to license.

Episcopal authorization is necessary to give Anglican legitimacy, to provide a framework of accountability, to maximize learning from what occurs and to encourage positive acceptance from the parishes involved.

All such decisions need to be made based upon the merits of each case, and as appropriate for each parish in the light of an agreed deanery or diocesan strategy.

Decisions also need to be made in the light of conversations with other denominations, so that what is proposed connects well with and respects the mission initiatives and intentions of those other denominations.

proposed fresh expressions of church need to work in ways that are complementary to inherited ways
Proposals for further church communities will include a variety of new forms or expressions of church. Anglicanism has long prided itself on its diversity and tolerance. Such diversity can affirm different strengths and weaknesses. An established church may have the strength of a known history, a fine building and established contacts in the community. But it might be weak in numerical attendance. A new church might have the vigour of a highly motivated and skilled team, but is likely to have an uncertain future, no settled patterns and an emerging identity.

It is expected that proposals will be developed for new forms of church that are clearly different from the parish in which they may be technically located. They would be unlike, both in terms of the types of people for whom they are designed, as well as the forms of church that are expressed. The different forms could include approaches in evangelism and wider mission, ways of being Christian community as well as styles of worship. It is also expected that the mutual affirmation of diversity would be the attitude towards which both emerging and inherited churches should strive.

existing ecclesiastical legal boundaries should be seen as permeable
The language of permeability reflects two realities. Parish boundaries exist and are a deep part of our history, the foundation of our pastoral organization and still contribute to local identity. They will not disappear and are still helpful. Equally, ever since the granting of Electoral Roll rights in the 1920s to habitual attenders coming from beyond the parish, the significance of 'parish' has shifted.

The notion of 'permeability' offers a framework for both respecting and crossing parish boundaries. The argument for permeability is the need for the Church's mission to engage with people in the way they live their lives in a mixture of networks and localities. The safeguards are the stress on diocesan identity, episcopal brokerage, complementary mission aims and the mutual affirmation of diversity.

an agreed process is needed to make these values credible
Before an expression of church across a boundary is begun, the process needs to be agreed with all involved – the leadership of the new work, the sending church leadership and the parish in which the fresh expression is

to be based. Change works best within frameworks that can live with learning on the journey, accepting the freedom to make mistakes, and using review as the basis for continued change.

One set of principles is suggested here, but these may be adapted as needed in the particular case. Implicit within this framework is the assumption that, as appropriate, plans will be developed with the participation of other churches with a missionary concern for the area or culture.

brokerage

- That a church that wishes to plant, or to develop existing organic growth outside its own parish, consults early with the bishop.
- That the bishop acts as broker between the sending church and the calling or receiving parish.

maintaining unity

- That prayer and listening to each other are part of the process as it unfolds, and that public prayer is offered by all parties for the others, on a regular basis.
- That the leaders and churches of the sending, sent and receiving groups maintain a consistent public affirmation of each other.
- That churches foster good relationships between themselves, expressed at appropriate levels and intervals.

consultancy

- That ongoing consultancy is offered to sent and receiving churches in terms of strengthening their respective senses of identity, call and mission.
- This consultancy will include issues of personal growth for all parties such as feelings of threat, fear of failure, jealousy and self-doubt, as well as how to rejoice in progress and how to avoid a comfortable plateau.

review

- A diocesan-led process of review is agreed at the outset.

The above approach has a number of commendable features:

- It maintains a unity that embraces diversity.
- It gives a missionary framework for diocesan-wide decisions, as well as practical steps through which to test out the process.

- It balances lightness of touch and flexibility with the need to embed decisions within truly accountable relationships.
- It is episcopally guided but also responsive to what is developed under God in both network and neighbourhood settings.
- It finds ways to match mission tasks and mission resources without being limited by parish boundaries.
- It seeks mutual prayerful affirmation that reflects holiness.

However, the above approach lacks one component that would enable it to deliver in difficult circumstances. What happens if a bishop is genuinely minded to authorize a fresh expression of church, but the incumbent or PCC declines to accept this opportunity, and protects itself with its legal boundaries?

the cure of souls that is mine and yours

In many walks of life those in authority have more power to say 'no' than to say 'yes'. It is easier to stop what isn't wanted than to establish what is wanted. So bishops may prevent disasters more easily than they can promote successes.

When a bishop or diocese wants to establish an initiative that crosses parish boundaries, but is faced with the reluctance or opposition of the local incumbent, there would currently seem to be little that can be done. The freehold safeguards an incumbent's future, and Canon Law appears to sanction his or her sole rights to the parish. The bishop appears to be able to do little or nothing, even if he wished to. Solutions may be found (including forming a trust that registers as a charity, and then recognizing that as an Extra Parochial Place) but it is the view of the working group that creative approaches such as these are not the best way forward.[10]

As the pace of network church picks up, so there is a growing need for a coherent and efficient method of enabling cross-boundary churches to develop. The urgency of the times and our nature as an episcopal Church means new ways must be found through amending the law to enable responsible partnership between planters and bishops, even if this means that the bishop has to exercise legal power over reluctant parish clergy.

finding the fresh lever for change

There is a case to remove one element of parochial power. Our suggestion is to request church legislation to change the canonical right to exclude the arrival of further Anglican churches whose creation has been sanctioned by the bishop in line with agreed diocesan procedures.

arguments against

These are bound to arise and need weighing.

- **There can only be one authorized ministry per parish.**
  Prospective incomers would be authorized by the bishop, so rightful order would be retained. The issue is not about the 'one' ministry, but the ministry being authorized. What is intended is the creation of more accessible diversity of ministry. In one sense all that is happening is what already occurs within a deanery.

- **There can only be one church per parish.**
  Ecumenically speaking this has not been reality for hundreds of years. Today ecumenical breadth tends to be welcomed as part of healthy diversity.

- **There can only be one Eucharist per parish.**
  Once again this assumes all other denominations' celebrations are not valid. Moreover, in a team parish, Eucharists may occur in various Anglican churches concurrently.

- **The parish church will suffer.**
  Experience in other provinces of the Anglican Communion has shown that the arrival of another Anglican church actively engaged in mission produces all sorts of contacts, some of whom are more attracted to the historic parish church. Thus the fresh church assists the growth of the older church.

This report suggests that legislation should remove:

- The canonical right of a minister to exclude further Anglican churches, where their creation has been sanctioned by the bishop in line with agreed diocesan procedures.

But affirms the wisdom of enabling a parish and its minister to retain all their rights to:

- The ecclesiastical traditions and style of worship of that parish, within Anglican norms.
- Real and actual possession of the church building.
- Security of tenure and continuity of ministry ensured by best practice of patronage and freehold.

- Offer pastoral care to any and all of the variety of parishioners within those boundaries.

A new balance needs to be struck. Protection of the parish and the ministry of its incumbent against unprincipled and unauthorized invasion is still required. Also required is protection of the mission of the diocese against prevention of mission by an incumbent.

why might this lever for change be important?

The case has already been put about the 'bishop in mission' and the unit of the Church being the diocese. This change is also entirely consistent with invoking the deliberately used phrase 'receive the cure of souls which is yours and mine'. That cure is not given away, it is only shared. In a time of profound missiological need it will be tragedy if legalism and fear of upsetting clergy prevent creative new initiatives. The mission of the Church needs to shift toward strengthening episcopal authority and reinvoking the cure that has always been the bishop's, for the sake of those outside the Church.

some questions for discussion

➤ What do you think is the best way to structure and resource mission? (Bible suggestion: Ephesians 3.7-13.)

➤ What can you learn from other Christian denominations in your area about organizing yourselves for mission?

➤ List the ways in which your deanery could respond to the need for fresh expressions of church. What things might your church do to encourage your areas and deaneries to engage robustly with church planting for mission?

➤ This chapter has identified four principles under 'how do we hold all this together?' that may guide the response to new mission opportunities at diocesan level:

Which of these principles do you think is the most important or significant, and which is the most difficult?

➤ This chapter emphasizes the need to identify, encourage, affirm, train and deploy people who have the gifts of 'pioneers', as well as those with the gifts of 'pastors'.

How can the ministry of pioneering church planters and evangelists be better encouraged and affirmed, and how can their gifts be better used?

chapter 8

recommendations

Mission-shaped Church looks at church planting and fresh expressions of church. It has attempted to give an overview and assessment of developments in those areas during the last ten years, as well as look at the changing nature of our society, and at what it means for the Church to be missionary within those cultures and networks.

A number of recommendations flow from these insights and experiences, and these are listed here under broad headings.

diocesan strategy

1. *Mission-shaped Church* should be studied in each diocese and at diocesan synods, with a view to helping shape diocesan, deanery and parish mission strategy.

2. In each diocese there should be a strategy for the encouragement and resourcing of church planting and fresh expressions of church, reflecting the network and neighbourhood reality of society and of mission opportunity. This strategy should be developed with ecumenical collaboration.

3. In each diocese an appropriate member of the senior staff should be identified who will be responsible for encouraging, reviewing and supporting existing and developing church plants and fresh expressions of church, and for their integration into the ministry of the diocese as a whole.

4. The four principles set out in Chapter 7 of this report, under the heading 'how do we hold all this together?' should be adopted in each diocese. Those recommendations are relevant in urban, rural and suburban settings, and are:

   - In any proposed mission where new churches beyond parish boundaries are in view, it is both right and necessary that the bishop act as the broker in discussions, with the ability to authorize a new venture or to deny it permission to proceed.

- Inherited ways of church and proposed fresh expressions of church need to work in ways that are complementary to each other.
- Existing ecclesiastical legal boundaries should be seen as permeable.
- An agreed process is needed to make these values credible.

5. Deaneries have the potential to bring together a range of human and financial resources, to consider mission across parish boundaries, and to share prayer and encouragement (Chapter 7). Each diocese should consider whether its deanery arrangements are best organized and employed to encourage the mission of the Church, particularly among people in cultures and networks not currently connected with church.

6. *Breaking New Ground* in 1994 contained guidelines for a staged process of transition to maturity and legal recognition for church plants. The latest version of these guidelines and the good practice they reflect should be adopted and used by each diocese. The revised guidelines are available on www.encountersontheedge.org.uk.

7. An appropriate process of record keeping should be established in each diocese, so that church plants and fresh expressions of church can be identified, supported and affirmed, and good practice and experience can easily be shared.

8. The National Adviser in Evangelism at the Archbishops' Council (or future equivalent) should serve as the focus person for the network of diocesan contacts (the member of senior staff in each diocese with responsibility for church planting and fresh expressions of church).

ecumenical

9. Local ecumenical cooperation is critical to the Church's mission. Churches need a light touch process that enables local mission experiments and partnerships between Christians of different denominations. A new category of 'locally-negotiated ecumenical partnership' (or equivalent terminology) should be created. The introduction of appropriate formal ecumenical arrangements should be delayed until the mission initiative has become established.

leadership and training

10. The initial training of all ministers, lay and ordained, within the Church of England should include a focus on cross-cultural evangelism, church planting and fresh expressions of church. This should be a significant feature of Continuing Ministerial Education (CME) from ordination through to years 3 and 4.

11. The Ministry Division of the Archbishops' Council should actively seek to encourage the identification, selection and training of pioneer church planters, for both lay and ordained ministries, through its appropriate channels to bishops' selectors, diocesan Readers Boards and training institutions. Specific selection criteria should be established. Patterns of training should be appropriate to the skills, gifting and experiences of those being trained. Those involved in selection need to be adequately equipped to identify and affirm pioneers and mission entrepreneurs.

12. First curacy posts should be established where church planting skills, gifting and experience can be nurtured, developed and employed. Incumbency or equivalent posts should be identified where the gifts of church planters can be valued and expressed.

13. A course, college or other institution with specialist skills in cross-cultural mission should be identified within each region, to provide key training modules and facilitate cross-cultural mission experience and learning. The resources of other denominations will make an important contribution to the overall pattern of the provision of learning in church planting and cross-cultural mission.

14. As part of a national policy, dioceses should develop vocational pathways for the identification, deployment, support and training of people with gifting in church planting, evangelism and fresh expressions of church.

15. The Church of England should develop procedures that provisionally acknowledge the work and gifting of existing and future lay leaders in church plants and other expressions of church. A pattern should develop that provides training as part of a process of discernment-for-authorization, rather than training subsequent to discernment, or the removal of existing leaders for training elsewhere.

- A pattern of training, mentoring and apprenticeship 'on the job' should be developed, rather than outside or apart from the mission situation where the leader (or potential leader) is exercising their ministry.

- Patterns of authorization for a specific task should be developed (for example, as leader of a church plant) rather than authorization with the assumption of a potentially lifelong ministry.

resources

There is an urgent need to release resources to sustain mission initiatives to the non-churched. The resources of the Church of England are understandably but disproportionately invested in inherited and traditional styles of church, which alone are no longer adequate for mission to the whole nation. Strategies are needed to establish new resources and transfer some existing resources for new initiatives.

16. In each diocese there should be established a 'mission growth and opportunity fund' (or similar title) – a fund to support new ventures in cross-cultural mission, evangelism and church planting.

17. In view of the Church Commissioners' mandate to provide 'additional provision for the cure of souls in parishes where such assistance is most required', strategic decisions about future patterns of financial support should be made in partnership with dioceses so as to help actively resource church planting and fresh expressions of church. This might include support for diocesan 'mission growth and opportunity' funds, and short-term support for the transition of some diocesan resources from inherited modes to church planting and fresh expressions.

18. *Mission-shaped Church* has identified that shifts in the population of England, and the large-scale development of new areas of housing, require national, regional and diocesan thinking and resourcing. The Church Commissioners in partnership with the Archbishops' Council and relevant dioceses should consider how best to resource the planting of neighbourhood and network forms of church in new population areas. Similarly, the Church Commissioners in partnership with the Archbishops' Council and relevant dioceses should consider how best to resource missionary church in areas of diminishing or declining population.

the Pastoral Measure and legislation

The subgroup reviewing the Pastoral Measure reported in 2002 that 'existing provisions in the [Pastoral] Measure cannot adequately or easily accommodate innovative church models'. The implications of this report and its conclusions should be incorporated into the legislation of the new (or amended) enabling Pastoral Measure. In particular, this applies to the recommendation from Chapter 7 concerning the retention of many of the existing rights of ministers, but the removal of the canonical right to exclude further Anglican churches, where their creation has been sanctioned by the bishop in line with procedures authorized by the new Pastoral Measure.

notes

introduction

1. *Breaking New Ground*, Church House Publishing, 1994.
2. *Breaking New Ground*, Church House Publishing, 1994, page v.
3. When this report refers to the 'incarnational principle' that underlies the Church of England's ministry it is not referring to the unique act in which God in Christ took human nature for our salvation, but the fact that the Incarnation took place through entry into a particular culture. This became a principle of Christian mission within the New Testament, and eventually went on to underlie the Church of England's parochial ministry, with its commitment to a parish church within each locality. See Chapter 5 of the report for a fuller theological statement.
4. See Chapter 5.
5. Revd Bob Hopkins. See Chapter 6.

chapter 1 changing contexts

1. Available from National Statistics Online (www.statistics.gov.uk).
2. *Social Trends*, p. 30, Table 1.1; p. 34, Table 1.7.
3. *Social Trends*, p. 42, Table 2.1.
4. *Social Trends*, p. 42.
5. *Social Trends*, p. 177, also see p. 178, Fig. 10.2.
6. *Social Trends*, p. 75, Fig. 4.2.
7. *Social Trends*, p. 75, Fig. 4.3.
8. *Social Trends*, p. 87, Fig. 4.26.
9. *Social Trends*, p. 88, Fig. 4.27.
10. *Social Trends*, p. 208, Table 12.
11. *Social Trends*, p. 210.
12. *Social Trends*, p. 21, Table 12.8.
13. *Social Trends*, p. 44.
14. *Social Trends*, p. 44.
15. *Social Trends*, p. 45, Table 2.7.
16. *Social Trends*, p. 22.
17. Chapter 2 of *Social Trends*, 2003.
18. *Social Trends*, p. 46, Fig. 2.10.
19. See the report on the National Census 2001 at www.statistics.gov.uk/census2001/profiles/commentaries/people.asp.
20. *Social Trends*, p. 45, Table 2.8.
21. *Social Trends*, p. 48, Fig. 2.13.
22. See www.statistics.gov.uk/census2001/profiles/commentaries/family.asp, also compare *Social Trends*, p. 43, Table 2.4.
23. *Social Trends*, p. 41; p. 51, Table 2.19.
24. *Social Trends*, p. 45, Table 2.8.
25. *Social Trends*, p. 43, Fig. 2.3.
26. *Social Trends*, p. 51, Table 2.19.
27. *Social Trends*, p. 227.

28. *Social Trends*, p. 227, Table 13.6.
29. *Social Trends*, p. 223; p. 232, Table 13.6.
30. *Social Trends*, p. 22, paras 2 and 4.
31. See also *The Search for Faith and the Witness of the Church*, Mission Theological Advisory Group, Church House Publishing, 1996, particularly Chapter 1.
32. Manuel Castells, *The Rise of the Network Society*, 2nd edition, Blackwell, 2000.
33. The term now used by sociologists to describe the dynamics of this type of culture. See Manuel Castells, *The Rise of the Network Society*, 2nd edition, Blackwell, 2000, Chapter 6.
34. 'The old model thinks of a culture as a "place" where certain things are collected together and ordered. But there is no such place. Our primary data are . . . patterns of flows and the structural forces which shape them.' Nick Couldry, *Inside Culture*, Sage, 2000, p. 103.
35. John Tomlinson, *Globalization and Culture*, Polity Press, 1999, p. 29.
36. The relationship between the network of the Internet and networks between people is explored in *Linked* by Albert-Laszlo Barabasi, Perseus Publishing, 2002. A key feature Barabasi notes is that both these networks have 'hubs' – in a social network this is someone who knows a lot of people, and may link different networks together. Some vicars see their role as being a 'hub' of the community. They are instinctively responding to the network society.
37. Ulrich Beck, *What is Globalization?*, Polity Press, 2000, p. 74.
38. Martin Albrow, *The Global Age*, Polity Press, 1996, pp. 156–8.
39. Zygmunt Bauman, *Society Under Siege*, Polity Press, 2002, p. 13.
40. Galatians 2.10, James 2.5, etc.
41. 'Social capital refers to connections among individuals – social networks and the norms of reciprocity and trustworthiness that arise from them.' Robert Putnam, *Bowling Alone*, Simon & Schuster, 2000, p. 19.
42. Robert Putnam, *Bowling Alone*, Simon & Schuster, 2000, p. 27.
43. Research based in the United States points to a reduction of social capital by 50 per cent over four generations. 'Members of any given generation are investing as much time in organizational activity as they ever were, but each successive generation is investing less.' (Robert Putnam, *Bowling Alone*, Simon & Schuster, 2000).
44. On 'faithfulness' see Vernon White, *Identity*, SCM Press, 2002.
45. *Breaking New Ground*, Church House Publishing, 1994, p. 3. It is perhaps also true that, in some situations, loyalty can become stronger to a place itself than it is to the people of that place.
46. See Chapter 4, for school-based congregations.
47. 'The difference is one of emphasis, but that shift makes an enormous difference to virtually every aspect of society, culture and individual life. The differences are so deep and ubiquitous that they fully justify speaking of our society as a separate and distinct kind – a consumer society.' (Zygmunt Bauman, *Work, Consumerism and the New Poor*, Open University, 1998, p. 24).
48. David Lyon, 'Memory and the Millennium' in *Grace and Truth in the Secular Age*, ed. Timothy Bradshaw, Eerdmans, 1998, p. 284.
49. Yiannis Gabriel and Tim Lang, *The Unmanageable Consumer*, Sage, 1995, p. 27.
50. George Ritzer, *Enchanting a Disenchanted World*, Pine Forge, 1999, p. 36.
51. Michael Moynagh, *Changing World, Changing Church*, Monarch, 2001, p. 32.
52. George Carey, *Planting New Churches*, Eagle Publishing, 1991, p. 24.
53. David Lyon, 'Memory and the Millennium' in *Grace and Truth in the Secular Age*, ed. Timothy Bradshaw, Eerdmans, 1998, p. 285.

54. Yiannis Gabriel and Tim Lang, *The Unmanageable Consumer*, Sage, 1995, p. 100.
55. Zygmunt Bauman, in Dennis Smith *Zygmunt Bauman, Prophet of Postmodernity*, Polity Press, 1999, p. 193.
56. This is discussed in Chapter 1 of *The Search for Faith and the Witness of the Church*, Mission Theological Advisory Group, Church House Publishing, 1996.
57. Callum Brown, *The Death of Christian Britain*, Routledge, 2000, pp. 193, 198.
58. *UK Christian Handbook*, Religious Trends No. 2, 2000/2001. See Chapter 3 for a fuller discussion of children's involvement with Sunday school and Sunday worship.
59. Bishop of Whitby, Gordon Bates, Church Army News, April 1998.
60. Brother Samuel SSF, 'Mission and Community', *Transmission*, Spring 1998, The Bible Society, p. 11.
61. *Church for Others and the Church for the World: A Quest for Structures for Missionary Congregations*, World Council of Churches, 1968, p. 3.
62. David Lyon, *Jesus in Disneyland*, Polity Press, 2000, p. 147.
63. Bob Jackson, *Hope for the Church*, Church House Publishing, 2002, p. 32.

chapter 2 the story since *Breaking New Ground* 1994

1. Source: database held by the Church Army Research Unit, The Sheffield Centre.
2. *How to Plant Churches*, Monica Hill (ed.), MARC, 1984.
3. *Planting New Churches*, George Carey et al., Eagle, 1991. Available from Anglican Church Planting Initiatives.
4. *Breaking New Ground*, Church House Publishing, 1994.
5. *Breaking New Ground*, Church House Publishing, 1994, p. v.
6. *Breaking New Ground*, Church House Publishing, 1994, p. vi.
7. George Lings, *New Ground in Church Planting*, Grove Evangelism 27, 1994.
8. *Breaking New Ground*, Church House Publishing, 1994, para. 1.6.
9. *Breaking New Ground*, Church House Publishing, 1994, para. 1.7.
10. Source: database held by the Church Army Research Unit, The Sheffield Centre.
11. For a missiological discussion of this in both the Hebrew Scriptures and in the New Testament, see the Mission Theological Advisory Group's *Presence and Prophecy*, Church House Publishing 2002, Chapter 9.
12. See additional material about church planting failure on www.encountersontheedge.org.uk.
13. *Breaking New Ground*, Church House Publishing, 1994, para. 8.2.
14. See Chapter 6 for a fuller discussion.
15. David Bosch, *Believing in the Future*, Continuum International Publishing Group/Trinity Press, 1995, p. 15.
16. *Breaking New Ground*, Church House Publishing, 1994, para. 8.4.
17. George Carey, Church Planting Conference address, 1989.
18. Examples include the creation of a diverse range of congregations using the same building, or groups that evolve, such as 'church' growing up around post-Alpha groups.
19. These include The Methodist Church's *Planting New Churches*, Methodist Publishing House, 2001 and the Baptist Union of Great Britain's *Planting Questions*, 2000.
20. George Lings and Stuart Murray Williams, *Church Planting Past Present and Future*, Grove Evangelism 61, 2003.
21. George Lings and Stuart Murray Williams, *Church Planting Past Present and Future*, Grove Evangelism 61, 2003, p. 25.
22. *A Church without Walls* is available from www.churchofscotland.org.uk.

23. *Good News in Wales* is downloadable from www.churchinwales.org.uk/cmm/renewal/goodnews.
24. Rowan Williams, *Good News in Wales*, p. 3.

chapter 3 what is church planting and why does it matter?

1. Bob Hopkins, *Church Planting: Models for Mission in the Church of England*, Grove Evangelism 4, 1988 and *Church Planting: some Experiences and Challenges*, Grove Evangelism 8, 1989.
2. *Breaking New Ground*, Church House Publishing, 1994, para. 2.4.
3. 1 Corinthians 15.37-8 (*Holy Bible*, New International Version, International Bible Society, 1979).
4. Some of these descriptions of new styles or patterns of church will be discussed in more detail in Chapter 4.
5. *Breaking New Ground*, Church House Publishing, 1994, para. 2.1.
6. *Building Missionary Congregations*, Robert Warren, Church House Publishing, 1995.
7. *Being Human, Being Church*, Robert Warren, Zondervan, 1995.
8. *Gospel in a Pluralist Society*, Lesslie Newbigin, SPCK, 1989, Chapters 10 and 11, especially pp. 118–122, 131–4. See also *The Household of God*, Lesslie Newbigin, Paternoster, 1998, pp. 149ff (originally SCM Press, 1983).
9. *Breaking New Ground*, Church House Publishing, 1994, para. 3.2.
10. For example, periods of adaptation and expansion in the nineteenth century reveal the desire to respond both to fresh understanding of Catholic thinking, and also the urbanization of society.
11. The missionary nature of the Church will be explored in Chapter 5 of this report.
12. Philip Richter and Leslie Francis, *Gone but not Forgotten*, Darton, Longman & Todd, 1998.
13. Created by inference from data in Richter and Francis, *Gone but not Forgotten*, Darton, Longman & Todd, 1998, p. xii, para. 2 and p. 138.
14. Richter and Francis, *Gone but not Forgotten*, Darton, Longman & Todd, 1998, p. 138.
15. Richter and Francis, *Gone but not Forgotten*, Darton, Longman & Todd, 1998, p. 139.
16. George Lings, *Living Proof*, Encounters on the Edge 1, Church Army, 1999, p. 13.
17. The figures for 1980 to 2000 are based on children's attendance at Sunday worship, not Sunday school. The actual number of children connecting to church through Sunday or midweek worship, activities and clubs is probably significantly larger than these figures suggest. However, even when these additional numbers are included, the total number of children involved with church and related clubs is still only a small proportion of the overall child population.
18. Lambeth 1988, Resolution 44.

chapter 4 fresh expressions of church

1. George Lings, *The Enigma of Alternative Worship*, Encounters on the Edge 12, Church Army, 2001.
2. For more information, see www.freshworship.org.
3. George Lings, *The Enigma of Alternative Worship*, Encounters on the Edge 12, Church Army, 2001.
4. Further information can be found in: Jonny Baker and Steve Collins, *Fresh Vital Worship*,

CPO/Grace; George Lings, *The Enigma of Alternative Worship*, Encounters on the Edge 12, Church Army, 2001; Pierson, Kirkpatrick and Riddell, *The Prodigal Project*, SPCK, 2000; Paul Roberts, *Alternative Worship in the Church of England*, Grove Worship 155, 1999; Pete Ward (ed.), *Mass Culture*, Bible Reading Fellowship, 1999.

5. David Prior, *Church in the Home*, Marshalls, 1983, p. 9.
6. Peter B. Price, *Telling It As It Is – Interactive learning for churches building small Christian communities*, New Way Publications, 1999, p. 5.
7. Peter B. Price, *Telling It As It Is – Interactive learning for churches building small Christian communities*, New Way Publications, 1999, p. 22.
8. Colleen Fleischman, *Essence of BECs*, an introductory outline paper towards the M.Phil., University of Wales, Lampeter, January 1995.
9. A full description of this development is given in a forthcoming book by John Summers from New Way Publications, *The Story of a New Way for an Anglican Parish*.
10. Further useful information can be found in: George Lings, *New Canterbury Tales*, Encounters on the Edge 7, Church Army, 2000; The Methodist Church's *Planting New Churches*, Methodist Publishing House, 2001 – the story of Café Church in Raynes Park.
11. Story adapted from CMS *Yes* magazine, Spring 2003.
12. See Ann Morisy, *Beyond the Good Samaritan, community ministry and mission*, Mowbray, 1997.
13. Further useful information can be found in: Howard Astin, *Body and Cell*, Monarch, 2002; Steven Croft, *Transforming Communities*, Darton, Longman & Todd, 2002; Bob Hopkins, *Mini-Guide to Cell Church*, Administry; Bob Hopkins (ed.), *Cell Church Stories as Signs of Mission*, Grove Evangelism 51, 2000; George Lings, *Has the Church reached its Cell-Buy Date?*, Encounters on the Edge 3, Church Army, 1999; Phil Potter, *The Challenge of Cell Church*, Bible Reading Fellowship, 2001; David Rhodes, *Cell Church or Traditional*, Grove Evangelism 36, 1996.
14. W. A. Beckham, *The Second Reformation*, Touch Publications, 1995, p. 29.
15. For cell church material see the Cell Church UK web site: www.cellchurch.co.uk.
16. Ralph Neighbour, *Where do we go from here?*, Touch Publications, 2000; William A. Beckham, *The Second Reformation*, Touch Publications, 1995. Popular English books derive their thinking from this model: Howard Astin, *Body and Cell*, Monarch, 2002; Phil Potter, *The Challenge of Cell Church*, Bible Reading Fellowship, 2001; Lawrence Singlehurst, *Loving the Lost*, Kingsway, 2001.
17. Howard Astin, *Body and Cell*, Monarch, 2002 and Phil Potter, *The Challenge of Cell Church*, Bible Reading Fellowship, 2001 are two English authors advocating 'pure cell'. Steven Croft, *Transforming Communities*, Darton, Longman & Todd, 2002 explores a Meta Church approach.
18. Paul Simmonds et al., *A Future for House Groups*, Grove Pastoral 66, 1996, p. 4.
19. This may not be so true of the Neighbour/Beckham style of cell church in North America.
20. Cell-based churches tend to be more relationship based and so become more network focused, whereas congregations with buildings, a history and their style of mission to the community as a whole tend to be more area based.
21. Bob Hopkins (ed.), *Cell Church Stories as Signs of Mission*, Grove Evangelism 51, 2000.
22. In some UPA areas there is a serious issue about access to homes being restricted to extended family only. A number of UPA cell churches have overcome this problem.
23. The reasons why English large churches have plateaued and even declined are explored by Bob Jackson in *Hope for the Church*, Church House Publishing, 2002, Chapter 11. This chapter specifically urges large churches to imitate some aspects of small churches (pp. 123ff).

24. See Phil Potter, *The Challenge of Cell Church*, Bible Reading Fellowship, 2001.
25. The Church Army's Sheffield Centre has gathered a number of papers and theses that address some of these ecclesiological and denominational questions.
26. See Ann Morisy, *Beyond the Good Samaritan*, Mowbray, 1997 for a helpful delineation of the rationale and practical processes for this way of working.
27. See Robert Warren, *Building Missionary Congregations*, Church House Publishing, 1995, p. 20.
28. An MSE is a Minister in Secular Employment, who earns his or her living in a secular job, but devotes some of his or her time to church work.
29. See George Lings, *Living Proof – a new way of being Church?*, Encounters on the Edge 1, Church Army, 1999.
30. For further information, see Ann Morisy, *Beyond the Good Samaritan*, Mowbray, 1997; David Evans and Mike Fearon, *From Strangers to Neighbours*, Hodder & Stoughton, 1998.
31. Peter Brierley, *The Tide is Running Out*, Christian Research, 2000.
32. *Vital Statistics*, Springboard/Archbishops' Council, 2002.
33. Peter Brierley, *The Tide is Running Out*, Christian Research, 2000, pp. 162–171.
34. This approach has recently been adopted by a newly planted congregation at Christ the King, Kettering.
35. *Transmission,* Bible Society, Summer 2002.
36. One example can be found in *Thame or Wild*, Encounters on the Edge 8, Church Army, 2000.
37. Bishop Michael Nazir-Ali, *Shapes of the Church to Come*, Kingsway, 2001, pp. 40–70.
38. See the 'Cell Church' section of this chapter.
39. See Chapter 3 for an explanation of the terms 'non-churched' and 'de-churched'.
40. *The Way Ahead: Church of England Schools in the New Millennium*, Church House Publishing, 2001.
41. For two stories, see George Lings, *Never on a Sunday*, Encounters on the Edge 11, Church Army, 2001.
42. The current national Church of England Youth Initiative, which includes the encouragement of more Church schools, is based on a view that 'Church schools are at the heart of the Church's mission'. There is considerable scope to develop both the implicit mission role of schools, and also their explicit role as Christian worshipping and serving communities for pupils, parents and friends.
43. See Ian Dewar, *Common Worship in Schools*, Grove Worship 174, 2003.
44. Chris Stoddard and Anne Hibbert, *Evaluating Seeker Services*, Administry Paper HTG 2:8.
45. The Reaching the Unchurched Network (RUN) offers useful resources and encouragement to churches in England looking either to develop Seeker Services, or to introduce 'seeker' elements into their existing pattern of services and events, or that are exploring emerging styles of church. See www.run.org.uk.
46. For stories of how some of these have fared, see *Leading Lights – who can lead new churches?*, Encounters on the Edge 9, Church Army, 2001.
47. Lee Abbey and Scargill are earlier expressions of this phenomenon.
48. For an introductory guide to The Order of Mission, and explanation of terms, see www.stthomaschurch.org.uk.
49. Held by one church in seven according to Peter Brierley's *The Tide is Running Out*, Christian Research, 2000, p. 162, and a potential growth factor according to Springboard's booklet *There Are Answers* (downloadable from www.springboard.uk.net).
50. Graham Cray, *Youth Congregations and the Emerging Church*, Grove Evangelism 57, 2002, pp. 13 and 23 make reference to around ten examples.

51. For the fuller story see *Eternity – the beginning*, Encounters on the Edge 4, Church Army, 1999.
52. From a paper written for Coventry Diocese and available at www.covdioc.webspace. fish.co.uk, or email mission@covdioc.org.
53. Source: *Statistics of Licensed Ministers 2001*, GS Misc 673, Church House Publishing, 2002. The average age of incumbents and assistant curates is 50 years.
54. Source: *Church Statistics*, Archbishops' Council, 2000. In 2000 there were 161,000 Baptisms and 36,000 Confirmations. In the 1980s there were approximately 200,000 Baptisms each year. In 1980 there were 98,000 Confirmations.
55. *Youth A Part*, Church House Publishing, 1996, p. 22.
56. *Good News for Young People: The Church of England's National Youth Strategy*, a joint report by the Board of Education and the Board of Mission, GS 1481, 2002, Section B, pp. 6–8.
57. Andy Furlong and Fred Cartmel, *Young People and Social Change*, Oxford University Press, 1997, p. 5.
58. *Youth A Part*, Church House Publishing, 1996, para. 2.11.
59. 3rd Academic Conference on Youth Ministry, Mansfield College, Oxford, January 1999.
60. Stuart Murray, *Church Planting Laying Foundations*, Herald Press, 2001.
61. Bob Hopkins (ed.), *Cell Church Stories as Signs of Mission*, Grove Evangelism 51, 2000, p. 3.
62. *Five Marks of Mission* from the 1988 Lambeth Conference:

    To proclaim the Good News of the Kingdom.
    To teach, baptize and nurture new believers.
    To respond to human need by loving service.
    To seek to transform unjust structures of society.
    To strive to safeguard the integrity of creation and sustain and renew the earth.

63. These also connect with the theological discussion in Chapter 5.
64. Today's English Version (2nd edition), American Bible Society, 1992.

chapter 5 theology for a missionary Church

1. *Eucharistic Presidency*, Church House Publishing, 1997, 2.2. Chapter 2 gives the most developed recent Church of England statement that the mission of the Church is to share in the mission of God. Our brief comments assume acceptance of that chapter, and summarize and apply elements of it. In addition, *Presence and Prophecy (a heart for mission in theological education)*, Mission Theological Advisory Group, Churches Together in Britain and Ireland/Church House Publishing, 2002 sets out an ecumenically-based affirmation of the fundamental place of mission in the nature and purposes of God and of God's Church. See especially Chapter 2, *The World as God sees it*.
2. See *Presence and Prophecy*, Churches Together in Britain and Ireland/Church House Publishing, 2002, p. 26.
3. *Eucharistic Presidency*, Church House Publishing, 1997, 2.6.
4. *Eucharistic Presidency*, Church House Publishing, 1997, 2.7. And see *Presence and Prophecy*, Churches Together in Britain and Ireland/Church House Publishing, 2002, p. x.
5. Stuart Murray, *Church Planting: Laying Foundations*, Paternoster Press, 1998, p. 31. And see *Presence and Prophecy*, Churches Together in Britain and Ireland/Church House Publishing, 2002, p. 25.

6. James Torrance, *Worship, Community and the Triune God of Grace*, Paternoster, 1996, p. ix.
7. David Bosch, *Transforming Mission*, Orbis, 1991, p. 390.
8. Tim Dearborn, *Beyond Duty: a passion for Christ, a heart for mission*, MARC, 1998.
9. Robin Greenwood, *Practising Community*, SPCK, 1996, p. 28.
10. 1 Corinthians 3.11.
11. Daniel Hardy, *Finding the Church*, SCM Press, 2001, p. 4.
12. Luke 1.35.
13. Hebrews 9.14.
14. Justin Martyr, *First Apology* 44 and *Second Apology* 9 and 13. The text can be downloaded from www.earlychristianwritings.com/justin.html.
15. E. Penoukou, *L'église d'Afrique: Propositions pour l'Avenir*, Paris 1984, described by Aylward Shorter, *Towards a Theology of Inculturation*, Geoffrey Chapman, 1988.
16. All references to the Incarnation, or to an incarnational principle, in this report refer to the culturally specific nature of Christ's Incarnation, as a principle for Christian mission.
17. See Lamin Sanneh, *Translating the Message: The Missionary Impact on Culture*, Orbis, 1989.
18. From the Decree on the Church's Missionary Activity of the Second Vatican Council, *Ad Gentes 10* in Austin Flannery (ed.), *Vatican Council II; The Conciliar and Post Conciliar Documents*, Costello Publishing Company, 1988, pp. 824–5.
19. Miroslav Volf, *Exclusion and Embrace*, Abingdon Press, 1996, p. 25.
20. John 12.32.
21. Morna Hooker 'Interchange in Christ' in *From Adam to Christ: Essays on Paul*, Cambridge University Press, 1990, pp. 13–72, and 'A Partner in the Gospel: Paul's Understanding of His Ministry' in *Theology and Ethics in Paul and his Interpreters*, Eugene H. Lovering and Jerry L. Sumney (eds), Abingdon, 1996, pp. 83–100.
22. Irenaeus famously made the statement that 'God became man that man might become God' in his understanding of Christ's undoing of Adam's sin. This idea was taken up by Augustine and later Aquinas.
23. 1 Corinthians 9.19ff.
24. Gerald Arbuckle, *Grieving for Change: a Spirituality for Refounding Gospel Communities*, Geoffrey Chapman, 1991, p. 118. As a Roman Catholic writer, Arbuckle uses the term 'inculturation' to indicate evangelization as involving a process of exchange in which the gospel is inserted into the very heart of a culture.
25. John 20.21.
26. See also 1 Corinthians 11.1.
27. 1 Corinthians 15.20-22.
28. Philippians 3.10.
29. 1 Corinthians 15.58.
30. 1 Corinthians 15.20, Romans 8.23.
31. 1 Corinthians 15.3-11.
32. The Spirit is the first fruits of the harvest that will be reaped at the end of the age (Romans 8.23). The Spirit is the down payment, the first part of what will be received in full when Christ returns (2 Corinthians 1.22; 5.5; Ephesians 1.14). The Spirit is the seal that guarantees 'the day of redemption' (2 Corinthians 1.21,22; Ephesians 1.13; 4.30). The Spirit is the present dynamic power of the future age (Hebrews 6.4,5; Acts 1.8; 1 Corinthians 4.5).
33. See *Presence and Prophecy*, Churches Together in Britain and Ireland/Church House Publishing, 2002, p. 26.
34. Lamin Sanneh, *Translating the Message: The Missionary Impact on Culture*, Orbis, 1989.

35. See Tom and Christine Sine, *Living on Purpose*, Monarch, 2002, p. 58.
36. 1 Corinthians 12.12-13.
37. *Eucharistic Presidency*, Church House Publishing, 1997, 2.28.
38. Report of the Lausanne Haslev Consultation, *Contextualization Revisited*, 1997.
39. Michael Nazir-Ali, *Future Shapes of the Church*, House of Bishops paper, 2001.
40. For the remainder of this section the term 'inculturation' will be used.
41. Sally Gaze, *St Paul and Inculturation*, unpublished M.Phil. thesis, University of Birmingham, 1998, pp. 4–13.
42. Sally Gaze, *St Paul and Inculturation*, unpublished M.Phil. thesis, University of Birmingham, 1998, p. 11.
43. Report of the Lausanne Haslev Consultation, *Contextualization Revisited*, 1997.
44. *Eucharistic Presidency*, Church House Publishing, 1997, 2.21.
45. Syncretism is a process in which elements of one religion or system of beliefs are assimilated into or mixed with another, resulting in a change in the basic nature of the religion.
46. Lesslie Newbigin, *Foolishness to the Greeks*, Eerdmans, 1997, p. 7.
47. David Lyon, *Jesus in Disneyland*, Polity Press, 2000, p. 145.
48. 1 Corinthians 10.24,31.
49. 1 Corinthians 9.19-23.
50. 1 Corinthians 9.16; 15.3ff.
51. Vincent Donovan, preface to the second edition of *Christianity Rediscovered*, SCM Press, 2001.
52. Ephesians 1.23.
53. Bob Jackson, *Hope for the Church*, Church House Publishing, 2002, p. 32.
54. Genesis 22.17.
55. Genesis 12.3.
56. Lesslie Newbigin, *The Household of God*, SCM Press, 1953, p. 25.
57. See, for example, the work of Walter Brueggemann.
58. 'When they saw him, they worshipped him; but some doubted. Then Jesus came to them and said, "All authority in heaven and on earth has been given to me. Therefore go and make disciples of all nations, baptising them in the name of the Father and of the Son and of the Holy Spirit, and teaching them to obey everything I have commanded you. And surely I am with you always, to the very end of the age.' (Matthew 28.17-20, The Holy Bible, New International Version – Anglicised, Hodder and Stoughton, 1984).
59. 'You will receive power when the Holy Spirit comes on you; and you will be my witnesses in Jerusalem, and in all Judea and Samaria, and to the ends of the earth.' (Acts 1.8, The Holy Bible, New International Version – Anglicised, Hodder and Stoughton, 1984).
60. Prior to Antioch, the Church also grew and was built up: 'Then the church throughout Judea, Galilee and Samaria enjoyed a time of peace. It was strengthened; and encouraged by the Holy Spirit, it grew in numbers, living in the fear of the Lord'. (Acts 9.31, The Holy Bible, New International Version – Anglicised, Hodder & Stoughton, 1984).
61. Lesslie Newbigin, *The Gospel in a Pluralist Society*, SPCK, 1989, p. 121.
62. *Eucharistic Presidency*, Church House Publishing, 1997, 2.12.
63. Matthew 28.19.
64. Robin Greenwood, *Practising Community*, SPCK, 1996, p. 47.
65. 1 Peter 2.9.
66. Stephen Cottrell, *Sacrament, Wholeness and Evangelism*, Grove Evangelism 33, 1999, p. 9.
67. Revelation 5.9; 7.9; 13.7; 14.6.

68. Paul Avis, *The Anglican Understanding of the Church*, SPCK, 2000, p. 65.
69. Robin Greenwood, *Practising Community*, SPCK, 1996, pp. 27f.
70. Paul Avis, *Church, State and Establishment*, SPCK, 2001, p. 2.
71. Quoted by A. M. Hunter, *P. T. Forsyth Per Crucem ad Lucem*, SCM Press, 1974.
72. John 20.21
73. Quoted by A. M. Hunter, *P. T. Forsyth Per Crucem ad Lucem*, SCM Press, 1974.
74. The five marks of mission were formulated in documents of the Anglican Consultative Council (ACC 6; 8) and adopted by the Lambeth Conference. See *The Truth Shall Make You Free* report of the Lambeth Conference 1988.
75. Daniel Hardy, *Finding the Church*, SCM Press, 2001, p. 238.
76. The Declaration of Assent is made by Church of England clergy at their ordination. 'I . . . do so affirm, and accordingly declare my belief in the faith which is revealed in the Holy Scriptures and set forth in the catholic creeds and to which the historic formularies of the Church of England bear witness . . .' (*Common Worship*, Church House Publishing, 2000, p. xi). See page 34.
77. Graham Cray, *Youth Congregations and Emerging Church*, Grove Evangelism 57, 2002, p. 13.
78. Stephen Cottrell, 'Parable and Encounter: Celebrating the Eucharist Today' in *Mass Culture*, Pete Ward (ed.), Bible Reading Fellowship, 1999, p. 58.
79. See Sub-Section 6, 'Being a Missionary Bishop in a Missionary Church' in Section II, 'Called to Live and Proclaim the Good News', *The Official Report of the Lambeth Conference 1998*, Morehouse Publishing, 1999.
80. Chicago-Lambeth Quadrilateral, 1888.
81. *Breaking New Ground*, Church House Publishing, 1994, p. 3.
82. Martin Kahler, 1908, cited by David Bosch, *Transforming Mission*, Orbis, 1991, p. 16.
83. Tim Dearborn, *Beyond Duty: a passion for Christ, a heart for mission*, MARC, 1998.

chapter 6 some methodologies for a missionary Church

1. See the Appendix – useful resources.
2. Contact Spurgeon's College in London, The Church Army College in Sheffield, or Anglican Church Planting Initiatives.
3. www.acpi.org.uk.
4. Robert Warren, *Towards a Theology of Change*, private paper.
5. Michael Nazir-Ali, *Shapes of the Church to Come*, Kingsway, 2001.
6. *Breaking New Ground*, Church House Publishing, 1994, para. 1.7, p. 3.
7. *Breaking New Ground*, Church House Publishing, 1994, para. 1.9, p. 3.
8. cf. Encounters on the Edge series Nos 1, 2, 6, 14 (see www.encountersontheedge.org.uk).
9. The story is part of *Cell Church Stories as Signs of Mission*, Grove Evangelism 51, 2000.
10. Some commentators would say that many people in England are now 'pre-Christian', not 'post-Christian'. 'Post-Christian' implies that they have once been influenced by the Church or gospel, whereas many people are now third or fourth generation without any meaningful connection with church or gospel. They are to all intents and purposes 'pre-Christian' – yet to encounter Christianity.
11. Donald McGavran, *Bridges of God*, Friendship, 1955.
12. Galatians 3.28.
13. See also Stuart Murray, *Church Planting: Laying Foundations*, Paternoster Press, 1998, pp. 96–108.

14. In particular with changing housing patterns, the regeneration of some city centres, and areas where parochial cover is slender or weak.
15. The exception to this pattern has been the Eden Projects in Manchester. See Encounters on the Edge 14.
16. These are an individual planter or couple, a small team (say 3–14), a larger group (15–45) or a plant where those sent out are already of congregation size (over 45).
17. Bob Hopkins and Richard White, *Enabling Church Planting*, CPAS, 1995, pp. 11 and 13.
18. *Breaking New Ground*, Church House Publishing, 1994, part 4, pp. 11–14.
19. *Breaking New Ground*, Church House Publishing, 1994, para. 4.4.
20. Popularized and perhaps coined by Revd Ian Bunting, and appearing in mission journals in the mid-1980s.
21. This is nearly always true, but there are cases of such strong links crossing a boundary with permission.
22. An example of a story is told in *Hard Graft?*, Encounters on the Edge 10, Church Army, 2001.
23. The best-known examples are the plants from Holy Trinity Brompton, London. Whether they are all transplants and whether they can display missionary creativity is explored in *Dynasty or Diversity?*, Encounters on the Edge 15, Church Army, 2002.
24. In *Church Planting: some experiences and challenges* (Grove Evangelism 8, 1989), Bob Hopkins writes about a 'seed' venture when he and his wife and a few others moved from a prosperous outer London location to inner city St Helens, Merseyside.
25. Similar Baptist ventures such as 'Urban Expression' are described by Stuart Murray and Anne Wilkinson-Hayes in *Hope from the Margins – New Ways of Being Church*, Grove Evangelism 49, 2000, pp. 9 and 13.
26. For more details see *Hope from the Margins – New Ways of Being Church*, Grove Evangelism 49, 2000, pp. 11f.
27. See 'Promoting a Common Core' by Michael Vasey in *The Renewal of Common Prayer*, Church House Publishing/SPCK, 1993, p. 81.
28. Now 'Church Mission Society'.
29. See Martyn Percy, *Power and the Church: Ecclesiology in an Age of Transition*, Continuum International, 1998, especially Chapters 4, 5, 8.
30. *Breaking New Ground*, Church House Publishing, 1994, para. 4.5, p. 14.
31. See also Roland Allen, *Missionary Methods: St Paul's or ours?*, Eerdmans, 1962. Ninety years ago, from the Catholic wing of Anglicanism, Roland Allen (1868–1947) highlighted the importance of trusting the Spirit of God to lead, enable and empower the people of God in the task of mission and especially in the establishing of new, independent congregations. He rooted his argument in the Pauline pattern of establishing churches.
32. See also *Joining the Club or Changing the Rules?*, Encounters on the Edge 5, Church Army, 2000.
33. cf. Graham Cray, *Youth Congregations and Emerging Church*, Grove Evangelism 57, 2000, p. 23.

chapter 7 an enabling framework for mission

1. *Breaking New Ground*, Church House Publishing, 1994, para. 1.9.
2. See Chapter 2 of this report.
3. Excluded from this table are 'detached parishes' (where a single parish comprises two or more separate and unconnected geographical areas) and 'ordinary districts' (in which representation is via participation in a shared PCC).

4. See George Lings, *Dynasty or Diversity*, Encounters on the Edge 15, Church Army, 2002, p. 4.
5. 'Resource Church' is the term used in Sheffield Diocese. It is similar to what might elsewhere be called a 'Minster Model' – a core church acting as a resource to enable the mission and ministry of other churches.
6. See Chapter 4 of this report for examples and commentary.
7. See the Church of Wales report, *Good News in Wales*. The latter story is told in *Living Proof*, Encounters on the Edge 1, Church Army, 1999.
8. Chapter 6 of this report.
9. See Michael Moynagh's work on the *Tomorrow Project* in *Changing World, Changing Church*, Monarch/Administry, 2001.
10. The relevant sections of Canons C8 and B41 are:

> Every minister shall exercise his ministry in accordance with the provisions of this Canon. (Canon C8.1)
> A minister . . . may officiate in any place only after he has received authority to do so from the bishop of the diocese. (Canon C8.2)
> No minister who has such authority to exercise his ministry in any diocese shall do so therein in any place in which he has not the cure of souls without the permission of the minister having such cure . . . except at the homes of persons whose names are entered on the electoral roll of the parish which he serves and to the extent authorized by the Extra-Parochial Ministry Measure 1967 . . . or in a university, college, school, hospital, or public or charitable institution in which he is licensed to officiate as provided by the said measure and Canon B41. (Canon C8.4)

> Canon B41 might be employed if a plant gained charitable status and a licence were given by the bishop. It reads:

> The bishop of a diocese within which any college, school, hospital, or public or charitable institution is situated, whether or not it possesses a chapel, may under the Extra-Parochial Measure 1967, license a minister to perform such offices and service of the Church of England as may be specified in the licence on any premises forming part of or belonging to the institution in question . . . (Canon B41.2) The performance of offices and services in accordance with any such licence shall not require the consent or be subject to the control of the minister of the parish in which they are performed. (Canon B41.3)

> Such Canons were originally designed to provide worship for the members of these institutions, not to solve problems of boundaries and network churches. But, on the face of it, the bishop could cite Canon B41 to allow a non-boundary church plant, if it operated in a college, school or hospital, or if it obtained charitable status. The bishop could license the minister even in the face of opposition or indifference from the local incumbent.

appendix – useful resources

useful books

Baker, Jonny, and Gay, Doug with Brown, Jenny, *Alternative Worship*, SPCK, 2003.

Boff, Leonardo, *Ecclesiogenesis: The Base Communities Reinvent the Church*, Orbis/Collins, 1986.

Booker, Mike and Ireland, Mark, *Evangelism: which way now?*, Church House Publishing, 2003.

Breaking New Ground, Church House Publishing, 1994.

Carey, George, *Planting New Churches*, Eagle Publishing, 1991.

Cray, Graham, *Youth Congregations and Emerging Church*, Grove Evangelism 57, 2002.

Encounters on the Edge – information about this series is available from www.encountersontheedge.org.uk.

Gibbs, Eddie and Coffey, Ian, *Church Next*, IVP, 2000.

Green, Michael (ed.), *Church Without Walls*, Paternoster Press, 2002.

Hebblethwaite, Margaret, *Base Communities – an introduction*, Geoffrey Chapman, 1993.

Hopkins, Bob and White, Richard, *Enabling Church Planting*, CPAS, 1995 (downloadable from www.acpi.org.uk).

Jackson, Bob, *Hope for the Church*, Church House Publishing, 2002.

Lings, George and Murray, Stuart, *Church Planting Past Present and Future*, Grove Evangelism 61, 2003.

Mission Theological Advisory Group, *Presence and Prophecy (a heart for mission in theological education)*, Churches Together in Britain and Ireland/Church House Publishing, 2002.

Mission Theological Advisory Group, *The Search for Faith and the Witness of the Church*, Church House Publishing, 1996.

Moynagh, Michael, *Changing World, Changing Church*, Monarch, 2001.

Murray, Stuart, *Church Planting: Laying Foundations*, Paternoster Press, 1998.

Murray, Stuart and Wilkinson-Hayes, Anne, *Hope from the Margins – New Ways of Being Church*, Grove Evangelism 49, 2000.

Nazir-Ali, Michael, *Shapes of the Church to Come*, Kingsway, 2001.

Potter, Phil, *The Challenge of Cell Church,* Bible Reading Fellowship, 2001.

Price, Peter and Hinton, Jeanne, *Changing Communities*, Churches Together in Britain and Ireland, 2003.

Roxburgh, Alan J., *The Missionary Congregation, Leadership and Liminality*, Trinity Press, 1997.
Ward, Pete, *Liquid Church*, Paternoster Press, 2002.

useful material from other churches

Church without Walls (Church of Scotland) is downloadable from www.churchwithoutwalls.org.uk.
Good News in Wales (Church of Wales) is downloadable from www.churchinwales.org.uk/cmm/renewal/goodnews.
Planting New Churches, Methodist Publishing House, 2001.
Planting Questions (Baptist Union of Great Britain) is downloadable from www.baptist.org.uk/downloads.htm.
Stopping the Rot! (video and workbook), Methodist Church Publishing, 1997.

useful web sites

Alternative worship (www.alternativeworship.org)
Links to worldwide alternative worship sites, and access to resources.

Anglican Cell Church Network (www.accn.org.uk)
A network and resource for Anglican churches in the UK that are thinking about or implementing cell church.

Anglican Church Planting Initiatives (www.acpi.org.uk)
Advice, coaching and consultancy to Anglicans and others on church planting plans, policy and practice.

Cell Church UK (www.cellchurch.co.uk)
Encouraging and promoting relevant cell churches across denominations.

Emerging Church (www.emergingchurch.info)
Stories, reflections and discussion on the emerging church.

Encounters on the Edge (www.encountersontheedge.org.uk)
The site supporting the Encounters on the Edge series of booklets, and serving the Church Army's Sheffield Centre in Sheffield. Additional material to accompany *Mission-shaped church* can be found here.

Resource – church plant training (www.resourcechurchplanting.com)
A consortium of agencies and denominations offering church plant training, in particular church for the variety of UK cultures.

RUN – Reaching the Unchurched Network (www.run.org.uk)
Encouraging emerging forms of church to communicate Christ to contemporary cultures.

useful training opportunities

The following organizations offer modules in church planting:

www.accn.org.uk
www.acpi.org.uk
www.cellchurch.co.uk
www.encountersontheedge.org.uk
www.htb.org.uk
www.matterseyhall.com
www.methodist.org.uk/evangelism/courses.htm
www.moorlands.ac.uk
www.ngm.org.uk
www.resourcechurchplanting.com
www.rpc.ox.ac.uk
www.salvationarmy.org.uk/en/Departments/ChurchGrowth/Home.htm
www.spurgeons.ac.uk
www.stjohns-nottm.ac.uk
www.trinity-bris.ac.uk
www.urbanexpression.org.uk

on-line mentoring

www.coachnet.org/

general index

Note: page references in italics indicate figures and tables.

index of biblical references